Moving The Chains: A Parent's Guide To The NFL Draft Process

Neil Stratton

© 2018 Neil Stratton

Moving the Chains: A Parents' Guide to the NFL Draft Process

All rights reserved. No portion of this book may be reproduced, stored in a retrieval system or transmitted in any form or by any means—electronic, mechanical, photocopy, recording, scanning or other—without written permission of the publisher.

ISBN-13: 978-0692190593

1st Edition

Published by Createspace of Amazon

To my sweet baby, Polly

Table of Contents

Introduction 1

Chapter 1: Getting Started 3

Chapter 2: Case Studies On Parents Of Players 22

Chapter 3: Scouts 32

Chapter 4: Agents 42

Chapter 5: Interviews With Former Agents 62

Chapter 6: All-Star Games 70

Chapter 7: Combine Prep 89

Chapter 8: The Combine... 105

Chapter 9: Evaluation 110

Chapter 10: March And April... 117

Chapter 11: Other Leagues And Non-NFL Football Ventures.. 142

Afterword 150

Introduction

If you're reading this book, you're either hoping to be selected in the NFL draft someday or you're the parent of a young man who hopes to be. Before we go farther, I want to take a moment to introduce myself.

Who is Neil Stratton?: Very briefly, I've run a service called **Inside the League** (ITL) since 2002. It's a consulting service for the college and pro football industry. I played football at the Naval Academy in the 1990s; ran the 2008 Hula Bowl as its Executive Director; and currently work with the representation, financial planners, combine trainers, school compliance officials, or others associated with 60-70 percent of active NFL players. I'm *not* an agent, and have never been one. But I feel I know more about agencies and agent recruiting than anyone in the football business. Check out Inside the League's YouTube channel to get a better feel for what I do and what kinds of subjects I talk about regularly.

About this book: I wrote this book to dispel a lot of the myths about agents and agencies. There's a lot of misinformation put out by bad agents and sometimes by well-meaning people. I'm interested in cleaning that up. In the next hundred pages or so, I'll detail the entire NFL draft process, soup to nuts, for NFL hopefuls. I'll also talk about the agent business in some detail and with a critical eye. My goal is to make sure the readers of this book don't make any mistakes due to being misinformed or misunderstood.

Is it 'safe' to read this book?: Obviously, no one's ever lost their eligibility because they read a book, but there's a bigger issue at hand. I encourage you to give a copy of this book to anyone you feel might be interested in the process and who might be helping your son reach his NFL goals. This is important: in the pages of this book, I will never advise you to do anything illegal or outside the rules set forth by your son's school, coaches, or others.

Now, let's get going.

Chapter 1
Getting Started

This may be a little elementary, but we wanted to set the table by providing a quick overview of the schedule for draft hopefuls from summer until April, when the draft takes place.

August: NFL scouts are in camp with their teams, evaluating their own rosters so they'll know what their needs are. Established agents among the 800-plus registered with the NFLPA are building relationships with top prospects, while those who took the exam in July await test results. Some "street runners" approach top players. Many players and their families make a preliminary decision on their agent finalists, and some will even make their final choices before the season starts.

September/October/November: As the college season gains steam, NFL teams send staffs of 4-10 road scouts all over the nation. The veteran scouts are concentrated in the Southeast, Midwest and Southwest, and less seasoned scouts in the Northeast and Northwest. In September, those who took the agent test in July begin to receive their results and pay their dues. Prospects and their parents begin to whittle down their agent field and schedule final meetings. Representatives from the top college all-star games canvas the nation, with some games publishing watch lists. Invitees to the bigger games start getting their invitations in October and November.

December: NFL scouts return to their teams, compare notes, and begin to assemble their draft boards before fanning out again for bowl season. Non-bowl FBS players and non-playoff FCS players who were recruited by agents start to sign. Those who weren't recruited begin calling agents, hoping to sign with one. The Senior Bowl and Shrine Game begin publishing the names of players who are confirmed for their respective games, while the other games vie for the best of the rest. A handful of "self-sponsored" all-star games (i.e., pay to play) are played this month with mostly DII, NAIA and DIII players. The last week of this month, National Football Scouting (NFS) begins notifying "first-wave" players (around 250 seniors) to the NFL combine. It wasn't long ago that this list was passed around among scouts and agents in early January, but the character and arrest-screening process is a lot tougher now.

January: This is when the "pre-draft season" really begins in earnest. By the end of this month, 300-500 players will have played in major all-star games attended by NFL personnel. Also, by February, about 95 percent of all top NFL prospects will have signed with agents. The second wave of combine invitees (around 100 players, including top juniors who've entered the draft) is notified. Finally, combine prep facilities welcome players, with the kickoff of training season beginning the first Monday in January.

February: Early this month, NFS announces its complete list of around 350 invitees. Combine prep continues before the combine takes place at the end of the month. The first terminations of agents occur.

By the end of the first week of February, all-star play is completed. NFL teams assemble their pre-combine draft boards, then descend on Indianapolis.

March: "Pro days" take place across America, and about 2,500 seniors and declared underclassmen are evaluated in a series of drills by scouts on their own campuses. NFL teams finalize their draft boards. This is probably the most critical month for players as most evaluation is completed and final grades are awarded. NFL teams begin inviting selected players (up to 30) in to their respective offices for an extended look.

April: Top 30 visits continue in earnest the first three weeks of the month, and the NFL combine invites selected players back to Indianapolis for medical rechecks. The NFL Draft takes place over three days at the end of the month. For about 72 hours after the draft, NFL teams fill in their 90-man rosters with undrafted free agents and "tryout" players invited in for consideration a undrafted signees.

ROSTER UPS AND DOWNS

Obviously, the demand for players rises and falls throughout the calendar year. For instance, on the last weekend in August, NFL dreams end for more than 1,000 young men as teams cut from 90 to 53 slots. Though practice squads pull some of them back onto teams, the vast majority of those cut never play an NFL regular-season down. It's around this time that many players wonder, what's next for me, and how did I get here? Here's an overview of the league calendar in an attempt to answer these questions.

NFL: The league year officially kicks off in March, followed shortly after by free agency. At this point, teams have 90-man rosters, though most teams live around 65-75 players at any given time pre-draft. On draft day, most teams select 7-8 players, then add another 10-12 undrafted free agents, getting them to near the 90 limit. Most teams will leave 2-3 roster spots open after the addition of draftees and undrafted free agents, and invite 10-12 unsigned, undrafted players in to vie for 1-2 roster spots. They arrive for rookie mini-camp the week after the draft and go through drills in shorts and helmets for a few days, and based on their performances, some are signed. These are called tryout players, or three-day mini-camp players. From May through the start of camps in early July, there is minor roster flux, but things are relatively stable. Then camps arrive, and rosters turn over a bit due to injuries, etc., before big cuts are made in late August. After everyone has reduced to 53, teams are allowed to add a 10-man practice squad. After the season is completed, rosters expand again and teams are allowed to add players to "futures" deals. Players aren't paid for such deals; they only get the status of being part of a team, and are allowed to practice and work out with the team.

CFL: The CFL has a season that lasts from June (when training camp begins) through the end of November (when the Grey Cup is played). The CFL draft is the weekend after the NFL draft (around mid-May), followed shortly after by mini-camps, then full camps about two weeks later. CFL teams expand their practice squads in early

September, usually adding players who didn't make it through NFL cuts.

Arena Football League: AFL season kicks off with a two-week mini-camp and the start of the season in March, and it continues through mid-August. Like the other leagues, AFL teams are constantly adding and dropping throughout the season. Unlike the other leagues, there is very little activity for veteran players during the offseason. At that point, most AFL teams are spending all their time conducting fee-based tryouts all over the country in an attempt to (a) turn up overlooked players and (b) make money. It's not unusual to have 50-100 players show up for such practices at anywhere from $60-$100 per player (cash only).

The AAF and XFL: As I write this in the summer of 2018, two new leagues are scheduled for launch: the Alliance of American Football (AAF) in 2019 and the XFL in 2020. Obviously, this creates new opportunities for players who don't make the NFL cut, but there are still a lot of uncertainties attached to both leagues. And this is to say nothing of the volatility of alternative leagues in the first place. The truth is, the AAF and the XFL, depending on their sustainability, could radically change the shape of all non-NFL leagues in the next 2-3 years. There are only so many viable football prospects, and the number of people willing to buy tickets to watch is even more limited, especially in a crowded modern marketplace.

Summation: Once again, it's critical to know where your son fit in the draft. Players slated to go in the top 100 picks will be on an NFL roster in September, barring a serious injury. However, for those who are on the bubble to make a roster, it's important to know a little more about the "entry points" for non-NFL pro football. Bottom line, players who don't have a roster spot in June– when the NFL, CFL and AFL are either under way or on the eve of training camp, with the other two leagues also seeking talent – should strongly consider moving on to other non-football ventures.

DRAFT 'GURUS'

Any parent who's ever Googled his son to determine what kind of draft buzz he's getting has come across hundreds of draft websites. Some are pretty professional-looking, and many have robust social media presences with thousands of followers. What kind of information can you take from these sites? Are they reliable? What kind of information do they get from actual NFL sources?

Who are draft 'experts?': The short answer to this question is, whoever says he is. Every young man (or woman) who wants to someday work as an NFL scout sees signing up for a Twitter account as a first step so they can start spouting opinions on players. It's really not hard to start getting lots of hits and even radio appearances out of it. It's a good way to gain a following and become known. But it's still a long way from actually having influence on scouts or gaining real information from NFL teams.

How reliable are draft gurus?: Some are better than others. Still, what you need to realize is that they all copy off of each other, and nowhere is this more the case than in mock drafts. Mock drafts are the bread and butter of the draft guru because they're so easy to do and because they're so popular. While they might gather lots of traffic, this is in no way a measure of actual legitimacy in the eyes of NFL teams. A "draft guru" can get cited on ESPN, Fox Sports or Pro Football Talk, and it's still nothing more than entertainment to NFL teams (if it's even on any scouts' radar screens). Chances are, if a draft guru is talking to scouts, it's the odd regional scout who only knows of the players in his area, or perhaps a team's director of pro scouting who responded to a mass email. The bigger names in the draft guru game, the ones seen on the bigger networks, tend to talk to people a little higher on the food chain because they have a greater impact. Based on my conversations with scouts, they mainly read draft guides and look at websites to make absolutely sure they're not missing anyone. With the rise of modern technology, it's getting harder and harder to completely whiff on a player of any ability.

What does it all mean?: Most people use the Internet to gather more information about draft prospects; it's easy, fun, and doesn't cost anything. But please be careful as you Google. The first thing to remember is that the people running these sites are entertainers and should be seen as such. This is even true of people you see on TV, who may have some NFL contacts by virtue of their place on a major network, but are still far from being real-life NFL evaluators. The second thing to remember is that you shouldn't put too much stock in a site when it says a player's stock is rising or falling. There is so much that goes into a player's evaluation that these draft experts don't see, or aren't aware of, and making an incomplete evaluation on a player can really sway the results. Don't be led down a path, good or bad, with incomplete information. If you really want to get a fair evaluation, talk to someone who's really connected in the league or still works in the league. At Inside The League, we regularly help with such referrals, and have our own scouting department made up of former NFL evaluators. They're not flashy, but highly professional.

THREE POPULAR QUESTIONS

I often talk to the parents of players about their sons and the situations they face, and a few questions always come up. Here are three.

I'm on a watch list for an all-star game. What does that really mean?: The short answer is, nothing. These watch lists really drive me crazy, because they titillate and mislead but really don't tell anyone anything. For years, the Shrine Game put out a watch list in September, and dutifully, schools would publish stories about their players being invited to the game. That's not true. It's not an invite. It's strictly recognition that the player is solidly on the radar screen, but nothing more. Games are in no way, shape or form bound to invite players from their watch lists. These lists earn games lots of hits on their websites and lots of tweets and retweets, but they don't really have any meaning. That's why I encourage the parents I work with not to get particularly excited about watch lists. Legitimate prospects with good agents will be found if they go about the process correctly.

Can I talk to agents?: This is the question that bugs me the most, and I lay it strictly at the feet of schools. Very often their whole strategy is to scare players and their parents off from contract advisors (another word for agents, by the way), financial planners and such, which to me is irresponsible. First, the answer: of course you can! There is nothing illegal about talking to agents, or financial planners, or anyone else, for that matter. Now, deciding whether or not to talk to them is a legitimate question, but there's definitely nothing illegal about *talking*. How else are you going to get to know the various contract advisors in time to make a responsible decision? I always tell clients not to take as much as a bottle of water or a ride in a car with an agent or other football professional, but talking? Yeah, you have to do it. If you prefer to wait until the end of the regular season, that's up to you. However, if so, spend all the time between the end of the regular season and your son's bowl game doing as much research and having as many conversations as you can. A draft prospect isn't well-served by getting to the end of his college career and saying, well, it's time to start thinking "agent." No, that time was months, or at least weeks, ago. I'm not comparing a spouse to an agent, but you spend months and years getting to know your forever partner, and a week getting to know your son's potential contract advisor? I don't think that's smart.

What about pay-to-play in all-star games?: This is an area where I've evolved. We'll discuss this later, but it's important to fully understand the particular game and its ability to really help your son before he commits to them. In the old days, most games that asked players to share in costs were not very effective. In the old days, these games were nationally broadcast showcases for excited fans featuring names like Montana, Marino and Dorsett. Today, most games are really just highly competitive practices designed for NFL scouts followed by an extraneous game.

Bottom line, some games are good, and some are a complete waste of money and time.

WHO'S CALLING? HOW ARE THEY CALLING?

When it comes to recruiting, it's important to know where the pitches are coming from – from trainers, agents, financial planners, etc. – and how they're coming in.

Who is calling?: There was a time when the only people calling top players during the season were agents. That's not true anymore. If you're rated in the top 100 for next spring's draft, there are a whole host of people who will be seeking to win your ear. One, combine prep trainers may reach out, touting the merits of training where NFL veterans or other familiar players have trained. This is especially true if a player is rated among the top 30-50 players. Two, marketing professionals may call, pitching the idea of signing a separate deal for marketing aside from the usual marketing provided by a player's agent. This is especially true of top-10 prospects who play any position, or top-50 prospects who carry, catch or throw the ball. And of course, agents will be calling. At times, this starts in a player's junior year, or sometimes even in their redshirt freshman years if they've shown immediate production. For others, it starts the summer before the senior season. For still others who might have successful senior years, agents may not call until October or November.

How do they make contact?: In the age of social media, most players have Facebook accounts and/or Twitter pages. This is still a rather popular way of communicating, though it's become less so as schools have started to monitor social media. Some agencies have gotten wise to the process and brought in interns – usually attractive young ladies – to initiate contact, then ease in their agency affiliation later. There is also often a person who is close to the team who can put agents in contact with, as detailed by former agent Josh Luchs in his book, *Illegal Procedure* (which I highly recommend). There are also several schools that list players' email addresses, and some even list a phone contact. However, the bigger agencies that represent players from a potential client's school or hometown will get a direct phone number from their client, or even have the player call them directly. One agency that is known for representing quarterbacks does a remarkable job of having its NFL clients contact players. In fact, I've heard of some NFL players who do such a thorough job that their "quarry" grow weary of talking to them. Still, this practice won't end any time soon.

Who are they calling? Most agents from mid-sized and smaller agencies will try to first establish contact with either a player's family or his school, for a couple reasons. It may be because they want to do things honestly, but it's probably just as much because they don't have a way (outside of social media) of contacting the player directly. Bigger firms don't have that problem; whether it's through a coach they represent on staff, or a player who's a friend of their potential client, they can make contact. Either way, most starters at Top-25 schools are communicating with agents or their representatives.

DON'T ANSWER THE PHONE

Depending on where a player fits in the draft process, there may be callers who are to be avoided.

Brand managers: Brand managers are not agents. They usually portray themselves as marketing specialists who also have an endless number of contacts in the game and who can recognize good contracts vs. bad ones. Many even have backgrounds with actual big-name athletic companies (Under Armour, for example, or Wilson) along with a smart website that touts their credentials. You may wonder why they're contacting your son, and how they're getting paid. Usually, once they win a young man's confidence, they take a fee from the agent who signs the player as well as the financial planner who lands his account.

Business managers: Business managers have a lot in common with brand managers, though they are a bit more legitimate. Technically, true business managers aren't operating outside the law at all (provided they obey the rules, don't offer payouts, etc.). Usually, they pitch themselves as advisors who can help in agent selection, financial planner selection and combine trainer selection. They usually also offer tips on what all-star games to play in (or if they should be skipped), and will usually tout connections with scouts that can give a player inside info on where he fits in the draft. Typically, business managers aren't going to get their money under the table from agents, financial professionals, or others who work with the player. Instead, they'll charge 1-2 percent of the player's total worth annually, though some charge as much as 10 percent. Most players rated in the first round will hear from business managers. They'll work to make a player feel insecure about everything thrown at them, and offer to provide a secure presence and a "shepherd" to guide them. Maybe that makes a lot of sense. The important thing to realize is that players will be billed by their agent, financial planner and marketing professional *in addition to* their business managers. At some point, the money adds up.

Street runners: These are the most questionable people in the business. Street runners carry no licensing or certification, and usually don't pretend to have any. In fact, if you're a parent, a street runner will probably do everything he can to make sure you *don't* know about him. Street runners seem to lurk most of all in the SEC and ACC, and are very, very common in the Carolinas, Florida and the rest of the Deep South. Rather than taking on a pure advisor role or coming across as a father figure, most street runners are at or near the age of players (30 would be considered old), and look to be more in the big brother/best friend mold. Street runners usually try to portray themselves as completely independent but very knowledgeable of the agent selection process; they come across as nothing more than an advocate who isn't looking for any compensation, only companionship, camaraderie and a piece of the party action. In reality, most street runners are either affiliated with major agencies that want to keep their questionable activities at arm's length, or are committed to getting a fat fee from an agency in return for delivering the player with whom he has developed a strong relationship. Street runners aren't just the scourge of compliance departments but also good agents everywhere.

NFL DREAMS

On a Saturday one October, I got a text from an old friend, Ryan. Though he's one of my two best friends, we rarely talk unless he's in an argument and needs someone to help him settle it. In fact, his exact text was, "Call if you have a chance. Need to settle an argument." It was minutes until my son's birthday party, and I was rushing through Kroger picking up last-minute items, panicked and sweating with still several things on my to-do list. So naturally I called back immediately.

High hopes: Here was his conundrum. He'd been watching a game with friends and he'd gotten into an argument over how many college players arrive at school with NFL dreams/expectations. Ryan's contention was that only about half entertained thoughts of playing on Sunday; his friend said it was more like 90 percent. Without hesitating, I told Ryan he'd lost his bet. Then I told him this story.

Eye-opener: In the fall of 2010, I flew with a group to Phoenix. We were there for a news conference announcing the first-year Eastham Energy College All-Star Game, which would be played the following January. As part of our visit, we went to the football offices at Arizona State University. It was a lot of fun to meet then-head coach **Dennis Erickson,** but there's one thing I remember most about that trip: it was the wall outside the coaches' offices. The display was about 30 feet long and 10 feet high, and had on it a long, floor-to-ceiling frame. Mounted within this frame, taking up the whole wall, were half-shells of all 32 NFL helmets, gleaming and ominous. Beside each helmet was a list of every Sun Devil who had ever played for that team. It was incredibly impressive, and seemed to dominate the office. I immediately posted it on my Facebook page and remarked on what a difference it must make in recruiting. I remember one of the first comments under this post was from an agent client, something like, "every school has this in its offices." That was a real epiphany to me.

Silence: Here's why. I marketed ITL to schools pretty heavily in the mid-2000s and was met with a brick wall. I presumed that they didn't need me because they already did extensive work schooling their players and their parents on the league, how things work, and what their players' chances of playing NFL football were, etc. Later, I found out my presumption was all wrong. In fact, most schools avoid such instruction altogether.

The pitch: Schools tend to take a three-pronged approach to their players: (1) Keep your focus on the field, (2) you don't need to talk to an agent because they're all bad news anyway, and (3) all that stuff will take care of itself if you're good enough. To me this is horribly irresponsible. Still, there's a bigger issue. It's one thing to brush off the NFL when players are on their way out the door, but quite another if schools are using it to get players *in* the door, as most schools do. Clearly, players who might not have thought they were NFL caliber are, at the least, being given that hope by schools. I'm not sure I'm in favor of paying scholarship athletes a stipend, as has become a popular idea. However, remember that wall of helmets the next time a school official somewhere goes on and on about "protecting kids," the purity of college football, and the homespun appeal of amateur athletics.

WHEN NO ONE CALLS

It's my sincerest hope that everyone reading this book has a son, brother, husband, or other person who signs with a good agent and receives excellent representation. Furthermore, I hope that the draft is a legitimate possibility for him. Realistically, however, this may not be the case. Here are a few things for players to remember if they don't wind up signing with agents.

Don't panic: I've spoken to dozens of parents who really struggle because, based on a lack of interest by agents, they are afraid their sons will never get anywhere near an NFL camp. This is not the case at all. In fact, very often, agents don't express interest until quite late in the process. At the end of the day, truly talented players will be found by the NFL, especially if they attend FBS schools.

Don't spend money unwisely: This is so important, because bilking young men out of hard-earned money has become a cottage industry in the football business. Maybe it's a combine prep trainer; maybe it's some pay-to-play all-star game; maybe it's a paid workout; maybe it's some cockamamie "scouting" service. Just be careful before you shell out those dollars.

Know your all-star games: This goes hand in hand with the above tip. There are a lot of all-star games – most played in December but not all – that ask you or your son pay a fee to participate. If you have to pay to play in an all-star game, it's not normally a game that scouts will attend, and if there are no scouts, it pretty much doesn't exist. The games in January will, with few exceptions, have generous NFL scout coverage.

Keep expectations reasonable: Players who are ignored by agents until late in the process shouldn't cling to dreams of getting high-end combine training. Many players just use this as a paid vacation, anyway. Other frivolous demands placed on agents include stipends, rental cars, etc. If you're in this situation in November and December, start mapping out a training strategy at a solid local gym or at school. Once the season is over, take a reasonable break, then get going.

Focus on pro day: Even when players don't get all-star invites, they still have a final exam in their future. It's the school's pro day. Players that excel at their pro days can put themselves on the map in a big way. However, they have to do things that exceed others at their position at other pro days and maybe even the combine. They have to really show out, so they need to make their training count.

Publicity: One December, we featured New Mexico OL **Lamar Bratton** on our *Succeed in Football* blog, which is pretty widely read by agents all over the country. Lamar went from no agent interest to 5-6 calls in the space of 48 hours. We can't do this for everyone, obviously, but players who can find a legitimate platform read by agents can often get attention they otherwise would not have had.

FEAR

If you're around college football, you might sense a fear that schools tend to convey. It's a fear of agents, of all-star games, and generally, of preparing for the NFL. Many college programs spend four years infusing this fear into their players.

Examples abound: Every year, I see dedicated young men with late-round/undrafted free agent (UDFA) ratings playing for bowl-bound teams, and they wonder what they need to do to enhance their NFL prospects. In almost every case, I see schools aggressively working to keep their players in the dark. One year, the parents of a local player absolutely refused to speak to me or answer my emails offering to help, even though they shared my hometown. In another, a player's mother and sister both approached his position coach, pleading for any information on invitations to postseason games, and were waved off, with the coaches intimating that anything less than a focus on the bowl game would be practically traitorous. Another time, a player's parents dutifully shielded him from any agent communications, and with just a couple weeks until the end of their son's college career, they found themselves initiating a crash course on what they (and he) needed to know.

Loyalty and disloyalty: I know I've already covered this, but it bears repeating. There's one question I always get from well-meaning parents: can we even talk to agents? The answer is *yes*, a thousand times *yes*!! There's nothing illegal about it. It's like asking if it's illegal to talk to a Realtor, or a stockbroker, or a pastor, or anyone who offers advice and counsel about decisions. What you *cannot* do is take anything of value from an agent, and that includes something as mundane as a soda or a donut. When you hear of players getting disciplined for something related to contract advisors (like NFL players **Reggie Bush, Robert Quinn** and **A.J. Green**, who all got in trouble for agent-related matters while in college), it's always because they were taking benefits. It's never because they were having a simple conversation with an agent about what he does, and what his plan might be for a young player hoping to fulfill his dreams of an NFL career. I'm not suggesting a parent shouldn't be involved – on the contrary, I encourage it – but a player cannot be afraid of contract advisors. How else can information be gained? Loyalty to your school and your head coach is important, but it's also a two-way street.

Education: Here's what I always say to schools that try to shame/intimidate/browbeat their players into staying ignorant about the agent process: if you really value education, why do you devalue education about this process? And I'm not talking about big-picture-after-college-comes-the-NFL talk, but allowing players to learn the specifics of combine prep, agent selection, etc. All schools will be only too happy to tout a young man's entry into the NFL when it comes time for recruiting, but won't do anything to help him get there. This is more than an ignorant paradox; it's hypocrisy. Get educated. Please. It's your duty and your right. And that's what we do at ITL. Rant complete.

Chapter 2
Case Studies on Parents of Players

It's often more effective to let people tell their own stories. With that in mind, here are interviews with selected parents about their experiences during the NFL draft process.

2014 CASE STUDY: DON MEWHORT

Don Mewhort's son, Jack, was drafted out of Ohio State in the second round (59th overall) by the Colts in 2014. Jack started at left guard for Indianapolis for several years before numerous injuries forced him to retire before the 2018 season. Don accepted an invitation to receive our newsletter series on the NFL draft process, and we became friends after conferring throughout the fall on Jack's vetting process.

How much did you know about Jack's draft chances entering his senior year? Where did you get that info?: "We thought he'd be drafted, but we didn't have any idea where, maybe in the first five rounds. And where we got that information, we got it from various websites and media outlets. Ohio State didn't provide any resources for that. Ohio State stayed out of it pretty much. That being said, I didn't think it was appropriate to work through Ohio State on that. Given the history with agents and universities, I didn't think it was appropriate to rely on them for that."

How much anxiety or apprehension did you have about the agent selection process going into Jack's senior year? Was the process intimidating? "I don't think (my wife and I) felt any anxiety about the process. We only felt anxiety about the phone calls and texts that Jack was receiving (around mid-July) …. The way we handled it, when I got calls, or we got calls at home, we asked (Jack) to refer all the calls to me, and there was a process that we were going to go through, and we asked that they respect Jack's privacy and commitment to his senior season. We didn't really want him to be distracted. It can be overwhelming for the (players). It's flattering, and kind of like going through the recruiting process again, but I'm not sure it's in the best interest of the kids to be getting recruiting calls from agents during their season."

Did you have a lot of people who told you they could really move Jack up in the draft? "Some people would tout their relationships in the league and stuff like that; they know this guy or they're tied in with this person, or, well, you know. But we were pretty careful. Of the 10-15 people we met with, we were pretty careful. The ones we met with were all pretty professional. We were pleased. They were all very competent people."

What is the one thing – resource, advisor, whatever – you wished you'd had before Jack's senior season? "What would be helpful for parents is if the Players Association would put out the contracts from players from the previous draft. Like, 'here's what the second pick in the fourth round got in '12, and this was their agent,' because everyone brought in their own interpretation of the contracts. If the (NFLPA) could put out a consistent document that said, 'this is what everyone got, and this was their agent,' that would be helpful. We're probably a little different, but you got to find someone you can trust. You feel someone else can do it better, or a coach, or a lawyer, or an accountant, somebody at church, but somebody who doesn't care and that can help you with it. As a parent, you get a little biased, and you're probably not as objective as you should be. You should find that person who only cares about your kid, that can be helpful, and obviously the service (ITL provides) is helpful."

2014 CASE STUDY: GINA SWANSON

Gina Swanson's son, Travis, played his senior season at Arkansas before being drafted in the third round (76th overall) by the Lions in 2014.

Did it concern you that Arkansas' struggles, and the team's coaching instability, might affect Travis's status?: "Not in the least bit. In fact, when (former Arkansas head coach) **John L. Smith** came in as the interim two years previous, he really stepped up to the plate and told us everything was going to be fine, and being part of a team is picking people up and standing by the brotherhood they have. They struggled that year and had their challenges (during Travis' senior year), but Coach (**Bret Bielema**) was awesome, and we never had a doubt in our mind. We knew he was going to be just fine."

What kind of guidance did Coach Bielema and/or his staff provide regarding agents? "It was fantastic. For us as parents, having never been through anything like this before, when they had their spring game last year, Coach

(Bielema) and his staff put together a meeting of parents of seniors, almost like a little training seminar, and it was fantastic and gave us a lot of good info, things to expect, watch for, and plan for, and it was exceptional. We felt blessed to be a part of that and be more educated about the process."

Going into his senior season, what was your perception of where Travis would go in the draft? Where did you get that information from? (Laughs) "You know what? I'm completely honest when I say this: we had no idea where he would go. We could get online and read a lot of things, but it didn't matter to us in the least bit. We just wanted the opportunity for him to get drafted. There are a lot of opinions out there, and for every Google search you do, there's an opinion, and that's OK. There have been days (when it was tempting to search the Internet), but I think we made a decision as a family that some days were good days and some were bad days, depending on what you read, but if somebody wanted Travis, he would be picked, and for our own sanity, that would take us through the process. It was actually kind of fun."

What's the one thing you wish you had as an information source for the process?: "I wish I could say that there was, but I have to be honest with you. Up until that spring game meeting, we were nervous about going blindly into this and not doing the right thing. But (Bielema's) gathering (offered) so much information, and following (the ITL) newsletter was very helpful. It had some good examples, and it was very helpful, all the while knowing it was Travis' decision. Still, for parents, it was nerve-wracking, but it was helpful to have the education gathering that Coach B provided and the tidbits along the way from your newsletter."

2013 CASE STUDY: CARL LAWRENCE

Carl Lawrence had sons in consecutive draft classes. **Addison**, an offensive guard/tackle, played at Mississippi State and was draft-eligible in 2012 before going on to spend training camp as an undrafted free agent with the Ravens. **Cameron**, an ILB and fellow ex-Bulldog, was draft-eligible in 2013 and made the Cowboys as an undrafted free agent. He played three NFL seasons, mostly on special teams.

On a scale of 1-10, how knowledgeable of the draft process were you before Addison's senior year? "It would definitely be a 2 or a 3 at most. All I wanted was to improve his odds, and didn't want to do anything that would decrease them. I didn't want there to be hindsight later that I wished I hadn't done this, or had done that."

How much influence did you have on the process? "Addison chose David (Canter of DEC Management) on his own from word of mouth and after learning from that, I wanted a more methodical way of picking for Cameron. There's a difference there, in how reputable they are, how many clients, what his clients say, all that kind of stuff. Cameron listened to me and knew that I was doing my homework and he appreciated it, because he was so busy that he didn't have time to put into it. I still let him choose, but he had it all laid out for him." (Ultimately, Cameron chose Myrtle Beach, S.C.-based Turner Sports).

Did you use any advisors to help with the agent selection process? "Actually, no. I tried, but the (MSU coaching) staff was really busy and didn't want to get caught up in naming agents. They weren't that good at giving out info, because of the gray area, and you can understand that. They try to keep it separate. That's one reason it's so hard to get info . . . and by the time the kids are seniors it's almost too late to learn this stuff."

How helpful was MSU in educating the boys and you on the process? "They tried, but it was very limited and usually they didn't want to do it until the last game of their senior year, which is almost too late. It was just very limited compared to what I know now, but if we gave them a name, they did their homework and they could find out if they were registered with the school and the state, but any other info was very limited. I think there could be a better process for that. I know some schools have it, and that would probably be a good deal."

When did the recruiting process really heat up for you? "For Addison, it was a lot later, almost at the end, but for Cam it started before the season with basic contact with the agents. Of course, having the benefit of going through it with Addison, that might have put the exposure on Cam more, plus he was All-SEC."

What were you looking for in an agent? "I wanted honesty and I wanted to go by the rules, but I also wanted to find the information on how the process works. Everything about it, I was totally ignorant. I think it was a combination of the ones I could really trust and which would really work for us. I got so much info from (Inside the League) and it helped a lot, and hopefully this will get started. (ITL needs) to be brought into these schools."

2014 CASE STUDY: ROB BLANCHFLOWER

The son of Rob Blanchflower Sr., also named Rob, was selected in the seventh round (230th overall) by the Steelers in 2014. He spent the 2014 and 2015 seasons on the team's practice squad or injured reserve.

Did it concern you that UMass' struggles might affect Rob's status?: "It's always a concern. We were hopeful that being in a Division 1 program might raise some eyebrows, and as a parent, you're always pulling for your child, but you balance that with being at UMass."

What kind of guidance did UMass' coaches provide?: "I think they were OK. (Former UMass head coach **Charley) Molnar** had some challenges, and I don't think he had the connections with the larger programs and with other guys in the NFL that the more established schools could have. But from a standpoint of being encouraging and helpful, they were there."

What did you know about Rob's draft chances entering his senior year? Where did you get that info?: "As the season began going, it became more of a (possibility), and we didn't have the resources you would normally have, and that's about the time (ITL) reached out to us, and (its) program and (its) services . .. were very strong and a very good influence on what's happening and how the process works, and understanding the mindset of the agents, and what to do and what to talk about and what to think about. As it gets closer, you have to be prepared for that step."

When did agents really start reaching out?: "I think we had 1-2 guys really reach out to Rob even in the late spring/early summer (before his senior year), and we started getting some promotional materials in the mail. Nobody would directly reach out, but you'd get an email or something in the mail and 'congratulations on a great career,' and maybe one or two in June, and then we had three or four in late July/August, and then probably 3-4 guys again in August or September, and the frenzy probably was really, well, what happened was that the former GM from Dallas, **Gil Brandt**, ranked Rob as one of the top five tight ends in the country on NFL.com, and that was an unbelievable surprise for us, and once that hit the (web), we started getting people calling, and that, I think, was probably the first week in October, and then it started to build."

What's the one thing you wish you had as an information source for the process?: "If I'd had a crystal ball, I would have tried to learn more early on the process. I thought (the ITL) newsletter was very helpful for me, and those are the sort of resources you can really use. They helped me tremendously. I do think the schools could do a better job, and maybe the schools that have a better hit ratio do. If they had someone you could call and say, 'what's this all about?' that would be very helpful."

2014 CASE STUDY: RENEE FARRELL

Renee Farrell's son, Dillon, played in the 2014 East-West Shrine Game after a great career on the offensive line at New Mexico. Though he was highly decorated as a Lobo, he found December 2013 to be a little worrisome due to his difficulty in being seen. Though he went undrafted in the '14 draft, he signed with the Niners as an undrafted free agent and made the 53-man roster as a backup on the offensive line. He spent time with the Titans and Giants before wrapping his career in 2016.

Did it concern you that New Mexico's struggles might affect Dillon's status?: "Absolutely, yes. That was one of our main concerns. I just thought that perhaps (lack of interest from agents) was because they were struggling in the win-loss column... I just didn't know about it; none of us did, so we just thought, when the struggles started happening, that it was a bad omen that things wouldn't look good, though in Dillon's wildest dreams I don't think he ever thought he'd have a chance at the NFL."

What kind of guidance did the UNM coaching staff give you about the process?: "For us in particular, I don't remember hearing anything. We knew about some of the after-season all-star games but I would not say we were contacted by the coaching staff about those games."

What did you know about Dillon's draft chances entering his senior year? Where did you get that info?: "We didn't know really much about it. The only info we had about the NFL is when we started getting the (ITL) newsletters. We thought, maybe this is something he can shoot for, and we'll support (him) in anything (he wants) to do, and that's why the newsletters were eye-opening for us ... Just having the knowledge of what it was all about and what the process was, was invaluable to us. But we didn't even, I mean, myself, I didn't even know a lot about the process. You're thinking, "Golly, of course he's gonna go in the draft, and go high. He's my child!" But you just don't know, and if you don't know about the process, there's no way to understand where they might go."

When did you and your son get your first contact from agents and when did it get busiest? "He did have some contact unbeknownst to us. He had probably 3-4 people that were contacting him off and on ... What he told them was that he wanted to focus on his senior season, and would like to talk to them then. I didn't even know anything about it until we got to talking about it. He didn't want to chase them away but he wanted to focus and really wanted his senior year to be the best."

What's the one thing you wish you had as an information source for the process?: "I've (said) this: I wish we really would have had a resource like (the ITL) newsletters in maybe the spring before his senior season ... I don't know if schools are worried or scared, but if we could have had this heads-up that, 'hey, this could happen, I'm not saying it will happen, but this could happen in their senior season.' If we could have gotten (the) newsletters earlier on I think we would have been a lot better prepared and wouldn't have felt so behind."

Chapter 3
Scouts

NFL scouts have a job with intrigue and cache; almost every person who's ever won a fantasy football league has entertained dreams of evaluating talent for a living.

What do scouts do?: First off, there are two kinds of scouts, pro and college. College scouts are what most people think of when they think of a scout. They evaluate college players for the coming draft. Pro scouts evaluate NFL players on the 32 teams and "street" (post-college) free agents seeking tryouts, as well as the CFL and indoor leagues (and sometimes overseas leagues). Most teams have twice as many college scouts as they have pro scouts.

What do college scouts do?: College scouts are assigned regions – usually West Coast, Northwest, Northeast, Southeast, Midwest and Southwest, though teams split the country up their own ways – and travel 10-11 months of the year. They tend to live not where their team is based (necessarily), but usually in the middle of their region. In other words, the Seahawks' southeast scout might live in Biloxi, Atlanta, or Pensacola. Some perceive that scouts spend all their time watching college games, but that's not so. Many go home on weekends but spend Sunday night through Friday night on the road, visiting as many schools as possible. A typical day might involve showing up at a school and watching film all morning, spending the afternoon talking to coaches and team personnel about the team's best prospects, watching practice, then returning to the hotel to write up reports on the players evaluated that day. Then it's on to the next school, often that night.

Evaluation: Sometimes a coach will recommend a player, but usually a scout arrives at a school knowing who the top players are. Once a seasoned scout gets a good handle on the team's personnel (which may take more than one day), he decides which ones to write a report on, and which ones don't deserve a report. If a scout doesn't "write" a player, he's essentially declared him not a prospect even to be signed after the draft. The players he does write wind up getting cross-checked by the team's National Scout, usually a veteran with over a decade in the business. Most players that get ratings in the top rounds get evaluated 5-6 times by different members of the scouting department. The bigger, more talented schools usually even draw a handful of teams' general managers.

National and BLESTO: Most NFL teams subscribe to one of two organizations, called combines: National Football Scouting, based in Indianapolis, and BLESTO, based in Jacksonville, Fla. These two services employ scouts (usually young and/or inexperienced in the business) to watch juniors, grade them, and compile them in lists that can be presented to subscribing teams each May so teams can create their scouting schedules. They also time and measure players the spring before their senior seasons. This is how teams have a preliminary idea of which seniors to evaluate.

Where do scouts come from?: Scouts come from a lot of places. Some (not as many as you'd think) are ex-NFL players. Most played at least some college ball, though this is less common than it used to be. Many are ex-college coaches that knew someone and got their break that way. Many are family members of someone in team ownership. But the thing to understand is that scouts are getting younger and younger, and often making less money, because teams see scouts as replaceable. The trend now is centralized decision-making, and teams are asking their low-level scouts to go out and gather information like 40 times, stats and criminal histories, then let the GM and his inner circle form opinions and make evaluations. They don't want opinions from their area scouts as much as they want cold, hard facts. That's made scouting, which has always been subjective, an even more inexact science despite the fact that everyone on the Internet, it seems, is evaluating players today. You also have to figure in the impact of sports analytics, as teams have tried to identify trends and attributes that can define future stars by numbers generated in workouts, not on the field. Both of these trends have had a big impact on scouts' job security.

Job security: As we mentioned, a lot of teams see scouts as almost dispensable, and that's why a team usually brings in a new scout on a sort of three-year probationary period. If he doesn't seem to "get it," or maybe isn't thorough enough, or doesn't click with his boss, he may be tossed aside. There are also 'regime changes' that cost scouts their jobs. In modern pro football, turnover has become almost as common among general managers as among head coaches. To a GM, the scouting staff is akin to a head coach's coaching staff. In other words, there are people he's comfortable working with and trusts. That's why every May, right after the draft, there are dozens of changes to teams' scouting staffs. For example, we tracked 142 changes in staffs that took place in the NFL between the start of May and the end of July in 2013. That number is a little high. The over-under on front office changes is usually around a hundred terminations, promotions, transitions and other moves among scouts.

No right or wrong answers: There's a perception that there's a "black-and-white" nature to scouting, and that a good scout, if given the chance, can see obvious flaws that diminish a player, or big pluses that show that a player has talent and potential. Nothing could be further from the truth. Evaluation is a function of a player's talent, of course, and his pure physical ability, but also the skills and experience level of the scout evaluating him; how his school used him; the player's medical history; how his head coach or position coach felt about him; NFL team needs; local affiliation; and at times even the personal histories of the scouts themselves. There's also a lot of luck involved. This is why you have to understand that if one team rates a player as marginal, that's just one of 32 opinions that count. There are a lot of reasons a team might not like a player, but that doesn't mean a separate team might not love the same player. As in life, beauty is in the eye of the beholder.

OVERLOOKED

Here's a question I get all the time: how do players slip through the cracks? How do players go undrafted, then wind up having Pro Bowl careers?

Priest Holmes, Kurt Warner, James Harrison, Tony Romo, Arian Foster, Wes Welker and **Antonio Gates** are among players who, despite advanced modern evaluation, extensive media coverage and teams of evaluators scouring the country 11 months out of the year, were not drafted but went on to stardom in the league.

I asked former Jets scout Joe Bommarito this question. He had an interesting answer.

"Nobody slips through," he said. "This is a misconception. No player is overlooked, not because of his school, or record, or position, or any other consideration. Scouts evaluate every eligible player for the draft on school visits. No rock is left unturned.

"Whether a player has a first-round grade or a free-agent grade on him, that is what he has earned throughout his collegiate career. There have been first-round players who have not lived up to it, and free-agent players who have excelled. It doesn't mean they have been overlooked. It just means that is the grade they have earned in their collegiate career."

I respect Joe's opinion, but I'm not sure I agree, for several reasons. I think there are biases that, at the very least, affect the grades players are given. For example, players from losing teams are often seen as less enticing by scouts. Some teams give more weight to the preseason grades National and BLESTO give players, and when schools in remote places don't have players with draftable grades, at times theses schools are skipped altogether.

There are players that come from out-of-the-way places that just don't get the same exposure as players at schools in BCS conferences, for example. There are also players like **Matt Cassel**, who was a backup at USC for **Carson Palmer**. Though he was drafted in the seventh round in 2005, 25 picks before the end, he has had a lengthy NFL career. His grade was affected by his low usage due to sitting behind a Heisman winner. There are also several schools that give limited access to their players -- Penn State was like this under **Joe Paterno** -- or whose coaches have no idea how the draft process and evaluation really work (and, yes, there are many coaches who don't know or don't care, even today).

A SCOUTING STORY

Bill Schwenk had only been in player representation a month when, during the 2011 season, he noticed a cornerback at Nicholls State in Thibodaux, La., named **Bobby Felder**. Felder had played alongside Nicholls St. CB **Lardarius Webb**, who was drafted in the third round (88th overall) by the Ravens in 2009. Webb and Schwenk had a mutual friend, and this friend insisted to Schwenk that Felder was a player. Felder had big-time stats but minimal attention from scouts.

How come? Maybe because Thibodaux is in swamp country in south Louisiana. Nicholls' main claim to fame is that every summer it is home to Manning Passing Academy. However, it is by no means a football factory, having gone 1-10 in 2011 and 4-7 in 2010. The fact that the team went 1-10 his senior season didn't do anything to help Felder create buzz. In addition, he wasn't written up by either of the scouting combines, National or BLESTO, going into the season. Of course, this was because the school didn't bother to have a "junior day," the time when the combines come n to time, weigh and measure possible prospects. If a team were to find him, it would have to go to campus and check him out, or at least see him in a road game. Players easily develop a rap as non-athletic when no one has a 40 time on them; slow cornerbacks don't play in the NFL.

It turns out that only three teams made it to Nicholls that season: Seattle, Oakland and Atlanta. Seemingly, none were all that impressed (though the Falcons met with Schwenk at the Senior Bowl to discuss Felder). Later, Bill asked a friendly scout why only three teams had made it to Thibodaux. "Honestly, they're lazy!" was the response. The scout told Bill that because Felder played at lowly and remote Nicholls State, scouts knew few GMs would ask about the school or its players. That meant they could cut the school out of their route, and most did. At any rate, Bill was a believer, and continued to recruit Felder. He only got competition from one other agent, a veteran who heard of Felder very late and tried to get to him through the cornerback's brother-in-law.

Bill staved off the older agent and signed Felder, but making believers of NFL teams wasn't easy. That's why he made a game film and started to send it out to teams. One of the scouts who saw his film was **Alonzo Highsmith**, who's now with Cleveland. Highsmith is known in the business for his keen eye and excellent insights, and he went directly to GM **Ted Thompson** and told him he had found a sleeper. From there, word started to get out, and by the end of February, there was buzz around Felder. It reached such a fever pitch that when the school scheduled its pro day, many NFL scouts called to request that it be rescheduled to be held the day before LSU's pro day so scouts could make both workouts. Alas, at his big day, Felder ran in the 4.6 range, turning off all but the Vikings.

The next day, Bill drove him to Baton Rouge to meet Minnesota's scout and defensive backs coach after LSU's pro day. His chances mainly extinguished, the Vikings were the only team that called after the draft in April. Bill quickly signed Felder to a contract as an undrafted free agent, and the Colonel cornerback beat overwhelming odds and made the roster. He lasted three years in the league before moving to the CFL In 2015. Though Felder is no superstar, it's just one more illustration that there are still sleepers, and scouts and agents who are willing to trust their instincts can find them.

SCOUTS AND AGENTS

The relationship between scouts and agents is tricky, and it's important to understand how information flows around the league.

Connections: Every year, agents and financial planners get certified by the NFLPA expecting some sort of special insights into identifying prospects, or at least a way to build bridges with NFL talent evaluators, but it doesn't come. Just being a certified contract advisor doesn't give agents inside information on top players; there's no secret website they have access to, and they don't have a password that gets them passage to NFL war rooms. I don't say this to denigrate agents or the NFLPA. It's just that it's important to know that merely having an agent doesn't guarantee a player a place on a roster or any kind of special guidance. An agent's access to scouts is a function mainly of how long he's been in the game and what relationships he's been able to build. Often, a when a player signs with an agent, he sees it as a coronation, a sign that he's NFL-bound. This is very much incorrect.

"Scouts are telling me. . .": Depending on the agent, he either has lots of contact or almost no contact with scouts in the summer. Some of the more connected contract advisors have excellent scouting relationships, while the newer ones rarely do. More established agents may get plenty of info on players, but at the end of the day, it doesn't really matter much until the games begin. At any rate, the whole reason that most scouts talk to agents is because they represent a player that scouts have interest in. From January until March, there's a good bit of communication between agents and scouts as NFL teams work to find out details about injuries, workout schedules, all-star appearances, contact info and the like. Come April and May, scouts communicate pretty aggressively with the representatives of players they have interest in, and completely ignore the representatives of those they don't like. I say all of this because players and their parents are often approached by low-level agents, or even runners, who seek to gain favor by claiming that NFL teams are clamoring after the player. Be very wary of this. Often, when agents say that they're "hearing" information, it's just something they found on the web and they're trying to curry favor.

More on National and BLESTO: Earlier, we mentioned the two organizations that give subscribing teams their initial lists of prospects. Often, when agents say they have inside info, they're referring to information off these lists.

Even though all information from National Football Scouting and BLESTO is proprietary and only shared illegally, these lists tend to fall to agents and people around the game (especially the BLESTO list). If an agent tells you that your son is rated somewhere, this is probably what he means. Don't get too encouraged or discouraged by these grades. These ratings are not the last word, and have a definite shelf life. The grade that either of these services gives a player during the May preceding his senior season often has very little bearing on where the player is drafted a full year later. In fact, there have been years when the top-rated player in May isn't even drafted the following April. These grades are strictly a starting point, and everyone in the league understands this going in. You should, too.

Chapter 4
Agents

Sorting out contract advisors and all the misinformation that surrounds them is one of the trickiest parts of the pre-draft process, but it's necessary.

Experience varies: The number of certified NFLPA contract advisors is fluid, but the total usually stays around 800 agents plus or minus about 50, depending on what part of the year it is. Around mid-September, the NFLPA announces the results of the certification test administered in July, and this usually adds about 100 new agents to the rolls. On the other hand, the deadline for paying agent dues falls in October, and by the time non-dues payers are cut from the rolls, the number stays around 800. During the summer when NFL rosters are expanded, about half of the agents on the rolls have at least one player on an NFL roster; once the season begins and rosters go from 90 to 53, that number is cut to around 40 percent who have at least one active NFL client (about 360 agents). Of that 350 or so agents, probably 80-90 have just one client, and about 60 more have just two. Only around 100 have 10 clients or more and can really be called "seasoned" agents, and these hundred are clustered in about 50-60 firms. The bottom line is, there are lots of agents, and all of them have passed a test proving that they know the basics of the Collective Bargaining Agreement, but a relative minority have a real client list. It's no surprise that the longer the agent has been certified, the better his chances of having a sizable client list. The true heavyweights of the business have been certified around 20 years. A player might not have the luxury of signing with one of them, and there are even perks to being represented by someone new, but experience isn't one of them.

Professions: For the overwhelming majority of contract advisors, no matter what they say, representation is a side job. We do an interview series with first-year agents every summer immediately before the NFLPA test in July, and each agent we interview has at least one player on an NFL roster. Though players don't get paid during the summer, and it costs a great deal to recruit, almost everyone we interview says "being an agent" is his only job. That may be so, but if it is, these agents must have saved up some money along the way, because they aren't making enough to support themselves yet. I'd estimate that no more than a third of certified agents are solely player representatives. That said, there's no shame in that. The agent business has lots and lots of down time, with very little to do most of the summer and well into fall but recruit.

Professions (continued): So, what do agents do when they're not working as agents? The overwhelming majority are attorneys, and most are criminal defense or personal injury lawyers. There's always debate about whether an agent should always be an attorney. I don't subscribe to the belief that the best agents are always lawyers, though it's nice when they are. Bottom line, every professional in the sports industry is connected to a law firm in some way. It's just part of doing business. When it comes time to pick an agent, make sure that relationship is in place.

AGENT TIERS

One of the things we do at Inside the League is track agencies, big and small, measuring their success as they transition from year to year, adding and subtracting agents and expanding and contracting their client lists as the game changes. It's important to know that all agents are not the same, and most are members of a rather distinct tier or subgroup. Let's discuss this.

The mega-agencies: If you look at our list of the top agencies, based on how many players each of the top agencies have had drafted since we started tracking things in '07, there's a definite division between the top 12 firms – one is now defunct, as it was absorbed into CAA Sports -- and everyone else. If your son is being recruited by one of these 12 firms, he's on a different plane than most other prospects in his class, and probably looking at getting drafted in the top 100 picks next year. Just look at the 2018 draft. Though it was a little different, as the top pick was represented by a very small firm, the first round was nonetheless dominated by just a handful of firms. These 12 agencies represent the elite tier.

The dwindling middle class: if you look at the agencies that are just outside the first 12, you'll notice that several of them had no one drafted in 2018. Several haven't had draftees for the last 3-4 years. That's because the business has changed drastically in the last five years, taking a sharp turn upward with respect to the costs of signing and representing top players. Contacts and client lists, though still important, are now less important than high-end training, monthly per diems, stipends and signing bonuses.

Risers: That doesn't mean some agencies aren't dealing with the new landscape, either by pouring resources into the business or being very selective in recruiting and finding diamonds where others see only coal. These firms are mixed in anywhere from 20 to 50 in our rankings, and are usually populated by solid agents at the top who either found a way to bridge the money gap with high-gloss investors or recruit wisely and build slowly. These agencies may not be especially sexy yet, but they're on the way up, and they're doing solid work. These are the agencies that have grown the most in the past five years. If your son is being recruited by one of these agencies, he's in pretty good hands.

The newbies: Then you have the newer agencies, many of them manned by first- or second-year agents. Many of these firms come into the business figuring that the barrier to entry is money, and they throw a lot of cash around. Often, they invest splashy training and other resources on lesser players, driving up the market for those players rated higher. This drives the steady-but-cost-conscious firms crazy and often drives them from the business entirely.

WHAT SHOULD YOU EXPECT FROM AN AGENT?

There are a lot of misconceptions regarding what an agent *can* do and *should* do. Here's my take on things.

An honest evaluation: We're starting here because it all begins with a true appraisal of where a player fits into the draft class. My agent clients tell me every day how hard it is to tell a young man how high or low he is expected to go in the draft, and it's only partially because it's difficult to crush a player's dreams. It's also because so many players and/or their parents expect agents to paint a rosy picture for them. All prospective draftees or their parents should make sure to ask a potential agent where the player is rated in the draft. The agent should also be able to explain, in detail, how he arrived at that rating.

An honest representative: There are a couple of things to do before asking for that rating. First, a player must be prepared for whatever the agent says. If an agent is honest enough to give a player news he might not want, realize that (a) his honesty and willingness to deliver hard news may come in handy down the line, and (b) no rating is final. Second, understand that only a select number of agents (probably less than half) talk regularly to scouts and front office personnel and can get inside info on where a player is expected to go. That means many agents' perceptions of a player's NFL chances will depend on what he's found on the Internet as well as his own ideas of a player's potential based on his awards, school, the position he plays, and what he's seen of the player on the field. Again, if an agent is honest enough to admit that "what he's hearing" comes from media reports and his own intuition, rather than trying to pass it off as something he got in discussions with multiple scouts, at least he's not lying to you. That counts for something.

Responsiveness and attention: This goes hand in hand with honesty. There's a good bit of "gut feeling" in this part of the evaluation, but it's important. I remember someone once told me during my single days to watch how a girl treats the waiter, usher, bellhop, and other service personnel, because that's probably how she'd treat me once the honeymoon phase of the relationship ended. The same is true for agents. This is a business relationship, and at the end of the day your agent doesn't have to be your friend, but he does need to be willing to take your calls in a timely manner and give you a reasonable amount of information during the process. On the other hand, it's important to understand that this doesn't mean that any agent will respond well if you're calling three times daily, asking "what they're hearing," or constantly asking for a little help (i.e., money) here and there during the process. You're going to want representation that will go to the ends of the Earth for you, but you also have to realize that every agent is a person, and there's a limit to what's possible.

Combine/pro-day training(?): A couple years ago, one of my agent clients who was on the circulation list for my newsletter series seized on an item about agent selection, inferring that I had missed something. After we texted back and forth a couple times, he signed off with this: "Actually, all any player wants to know is where are you going to send them for training." As sad as this is, there's a lot of truth to it. Though it may be tempting to see combine prep as the major service an agent provides, it's important not to fall into this trap. In some ways, combine prep has become a way for agents – and even their clients – to get very lazy about representation and the agent-client relationship. Often, players think of agents as someone to take care of the bills over the course of an all-expenses-paid four months of pursuing the NFL. That's a gross oversimplification and not accurate. Rather than simply focusing on combine prep, a player should first decide upon having representation (or not). He should think of whether or not an agent would be a good choice even if combine prep wasn't part of the package. Like any business relationship, communication, respect, and competence matter.

Nutrition and health: These go hand in hand with combine prep, but it's important to make sure an agent is aware of any health concerns and can address them. Whether that's leftover aches and pains or a lingering injury that's been ignored in the interests of finishing the season, a player must be completely honest and know that his agent will equip him with sufficient medical care. Likewise, players may need to add or lose weight. Most, but not all, training programs will include this, but don't take it for granted. Make sure that any concerns are addressed, and that there's a plan in place.

Promotion to NFL teams: It's often said that an agent can't get a player drafted, and that's true, but that doesn't mean an agent should take a hands-off, laissez-faire attitude toward his clients. This is especially true when a player has a late-round/free agent grade. Promotion takes several forms, and it's hard to say what is most effective. I have a longtime client who believes strongly in the power of video, and credits his own editing and film work for getting a small-school player drafted in the second round several years ago. There's even a former NFL player, LB **Andy Studebaker**, who was widely believed to have gotten an NFL shot strictly based on his YouTube video. However, more than video, simply getting on the phone and seeking out opportunities is a basic part of an agent's job. That may be calling around schools working to get a better pro day; calling NFL teams to get a berth in a team's workout for local players; or most importantly, working to get a player signed as a free agent after the draft. This is absolutely critical, and players who might not get drafted must grill all agent candidates on such specifics.

One disclaimer: We've said it before, but it bears repeating: no agent can get a player drafted. A good agent pushes to get his client opportunities, but he can't run, catch, throw or block for him. You want a contract advisor who's hungry and aggressive, but realize that even the hungriest agents can't email, cold call or text your son into the league.

MONEY AND BENEFITS

Obviously, rogue agents may offer illegal enticements, and we urge players, in no uncertain terms, to run from any agent who makes such an offer. However, good agents offer various packages *legally*, i.e., after a player's college career ends. We want to discuss it in a cautionary way that gives some perspective – and potential downsides – to these offers.

Per diems, stipends and signing bonuses: If there's one place where the agent-player relationship has changed drastically in the last 5-10 years, it's here. Agents – good ones, not selfish ones – always lament to me the fact that players today seem to see their most important negotiation as not between his agent and his new team, but between himself and his agent. Many players want to be paid not just to play, but to be represented. The quality of the representation is seen as way less important than the immediate gratification of "getting paid."

A case study: I remember talking to one smaller West Coast agent who is now out of the business after about 6-7 years representing players. He identified a player who he felt he could sign. The young man came from a solid Pac-12 school, was rated as a late-rounder or free agent, came from a good family, and was on course to graduate. One evening, the agent spent a long time on the phone with the young man's mother, and felt like things had gone exceptionally well. When he started to wrap up the call, the mother finally just came out with the one question she really wanted answered: So, what do we get? My friend was pretty much blindsided. It was going to take everything my friend had to get this young man properly trained, fed and healthy; taught in all the techniques involved in improving his 40 time; tended to during his pro day; and all the other roles (friend, advisor, confidante) that an agent fills during the run-up to the draft. But none of that mattered as much as the big payday that his family was expecting. I'll never forget the disappointment in my friend's voice as he recounted this story to me. This young man was truly on the bubble as to whether he'd make a 53-man roster, meaning my friend was taking a big risk investing training fees, etc., in him, but that wouldn't be enough.

The bottom line: Players rated in the top 100 players for the draft will be offered some sort of package. It may take the form of a signing bonus paid in cash when the SRA (standard representation agreement) is completed. It may be a monthly allowance of a few thousand dollars (called a per diem) *plus* a signing bonus, depending on where your son is rated. It may be a marketing guarantee, an advance of several thousand dollars on the money an agent will get him for off-field endorsements. On the other hand, your son's agent contenders might offer a stipend that can be used for training or as an incentive to sign. This is all well and good, but there are two things critical to remember. First of all, these various incentives are *not* an entitlement, and it's important that you have a good handle on where your son is going in the draft before you begin to entertain the thoughts of such enticements. Second, picking an agent based solely on what he offers is a great way to wind up with a guy you feel stuck with. Remember, an agent isn't going to make such an offer without binding a player to him pretty strongly (and on paper). If you decide the level of service doesn't match whatever package he has offered, it may be very difficult to sever the relationship.

Differing philosophies: Depending on what agent you talk to, all-star games are either critical or overhyped in the evaluation process. My opinion is that it's much closer to the former. Unless you're one of the 20 or so players guaranteed to go in the first round, you're probably well-served playing in a game. Of course, with only a few exceptions, only seniors can play, and usually at least half of the first round is made up of juniors, so if you're a senior, unless you're going top-10, playing is probably a good idea. With all of this said, a good agent should have a well-developed philosophy on all-star play and should be able to articulate it for you.

Staying on top of things: We'll go into the various all-star games later in this book. In the meantime, however, it's important to know that the landscape is always changing. In 2008, the last year the Hula Bowl was played (and the year I was its executive director), there were a total of four all-star games. By way of comparison, there have been anywhere from three to six in the years since. It's really important to stay current, however, as games are always changing hands, getting canceled, getting postponed or being created. From 2007 to 2014, there were nine games canceled that sent players to the NFL the season before. Typically, there are 4-5 games. This counts only games played in January; the number of lesser games played in December and March – most of them pay-to-play – are too numerous to count. Your agent should (a) be fluent about all of the games during the draft cycle and (b) be able to tell you which games matter and which ones don't.

Connections: Just as important as knowing *about* the games is knowing who *runs* the games, and having an excellent relationship with them. There's a perception that the invitation list for each of these games is cut and dried, with the top game getting all the top players, the next one getting the second-best 100, etc. Nothing could be further from the truth. While there's definitely a pecking order to games, once you get past the top two, it's a constant push and pull for the best remaining players. There are also peculiarities to each roster. When I ran the Hula Bowl in 2008, I was lobbied constantly, and I'll admit there were times that agents I had longstanding relationships with got the benefit of the doubt. It's important you know how well any prospective agent knows each game's key people.

Exclusivity: One increasing trend over the past few years is that players and their families expect their contract advisors to not sign other players who play the same position they do. While there's some merit to this, it's important not to overplay your hand. Players with a legitimate chance to go in the first three rounds probably have a reasonable expectation of this, and most agencies will even expect this. For example, a top-five defensive end may not want to take the chance his agency signs another player competing for selection in the draft, as agencies may focus on the hot hand for the prospect with more buzz and neglect the less sexy player. On the other hand, if you're just hoping to get drafted, be careful about making this one of your demands. Chances are, less highly touted players will be recruited by less-established agents who, though hard-working, have to take on multiple clients with the hope that one or two of them make rosters. If you get a good feeling about a potential contract advisor, don't force the issue. There are more important things. Here again, this is why it's very important to have an honest, eyes-wide-open assessment of draft status.

Interview training: There has been an expectation over the last few years that draft prospects need to work one-on-one with a former scout or team executive who can give pointers on the interview process. While this can be helpful, especially for a player who's insecure when speaking publicly or in interviews, or a player who's got a checkered legal history, it's far from critically important. If you're a highly regarded prospect, you might have agents who offer this as part of their palette of services; there may even be former scouts who call you on an agent's behalf for recruiting purposes. On the other hand, if you're not so highly rated, there may be few, if any, agents who offer this training. The point is, there are no secret handshakes or hidden passwords that will get you past the NFL vetting process. Act naturally, be honest, and things will probably take care of themselves. Teams aren't looking for movie stars, and they aren't necessarily looking for choirboys.

They're looking for players who can talk about the mistakes they've made and explain why they made bad choices, and convince teams that it won't happen again. Players who don't have regrets about previous bad behavior, or a commitment to change that behavior, will probably be sniffed out by scouts. On the other hand, a contrite player will usually win teams' confidence.

Pro days: Athletes at FBS schools will almost assuredly get a serious look from NFL scouts. On the other hand, those that attend some lesser FCS schools, or Division II, III or NAIA schools, may not get that opportunity and could have sparse (or no) attendance by scouts. In this situation, an agent needs to be willing to make some calls to try to find a bigger NFL audience. Not sure if your agent has a plan for this? Make sure this is a question you ask. A player who doesn't have scouts at his pro day doesn't exist.

SEEKING REPRESENTATION

With the season winding down, many players and their parents use the post-regular season, pre-bowl period to have face-to-face meetings with their finalists. But maybe you're not in that group, and if so, there's no need to panic. Former Chiefs LB **Akeem Jordan** had no agent and no interest going into his pro day at James Madison University in the spring of '07, and literally begged several representatives before someone finally gave him a standard representation agreement. He played eight seasons, more than twice as long as the average career (three-and-a-half seasons). Here are a few tips on how to find the best agent.

Know where to look: Start by checking out the NFLPA website, where you'll find a list of all certified agents. This list gives you the people who are actually licensed by the Players Association. Many times, you'll be contacted by people who call themselves "agents," but they're in reality just runners. At this point, you don't want to waste time with someone who doesn't really know what he's talking about. You'll find email addresses and phone numbers (usually their cell) for all of them.

Know what to look for: I recommend that you keep the barrier to signing low. Don't come in with an expectation that the agent will pay for your training. Don't have the expectation that they will automatically get you into an all-star game. Don't expect your agent to have dozens of active NFL clients, necessarily. You're looking for someone who will be your advocate, not someone who can get you the most dollars on your second contract. Just because you came into the season rated higher than your teammate, and he's got dozens of agents calling while you don't have any, doesn't mean you should be getting the same kind of action he's getting.

Think locally: Your best bet is probably going to be an agent whose base is near you geographically, because at some point you're going to want to sit down with him and discuss things. Remember, if an agent has to take a plane trip to see you, or drive several hours, there's far less chance he goes to the trouble of even researching you. This business is very expensive and time-consuming; it's easy to dismiss you if you're too much trouble.

Seek referrals: Find a teammate or a coach who can recommend a good person. Most players can talk at length about the agent(s) they signed with as well as several they considered, and can discuss why they chose the one they did. Take advantage of this.

BE PREPARED FOR AGENT INTERVIEWS

Agent interviews can be both exciting and an emotional roller coaster. When planned for properly, a player and his parents can avoid feeling confused, disappointed and frustrated by the process. This is not the time to forget critical questions or the details of the agents' answers. For this reason, I asked my longtime friend, **Deborah Dubree**, for some tips on getting the most out of these meetings. Following a few simple guidelines can help you stay clear-headed, calm, confident and focused. Deborah is an Ultimate Performance Expert and the CEO of ClearEDGE, LLC. Her "no BS" approach, delivery and training methods have attracted high performing college and pro athletes, including NFL players from the Ravens, Texans, Packers, Cowboys, 49ers and more.

The goal: It is important to recognize that this is a business meeting, not a social event. When conducted effectively, the interview should be two-sided. You are exploring whether or not an agent has the necessary qualities – values, work ethic, responsiveness and expertise – along with the right experience and drive. The agent knows the prospect's stats, technical skills and consistency on the field. The interview offers the agent an opportunity to determine if the prospect is worth his or her time, effort, focus and money. Bottom line: is this a good investment that can eventually be *sold* to a team? Welcome to the world of the NFL. Players are viewed as a commodity. This is not just the agent's point of view. It is a reality of business.

Level the playing field: Whenever possible, sit at a table. This can be a kitchen table, conference table or similar. This one simple action accomplishes several objectives. 1.) Everyone in the room will be at the same eye level. 2.) It just feels more like a business meeting. 3.) You can more easily take notes and use your notes (see **Keep Score** below) to ensure you have clear and concise information to make this important decision.

Your team: Players and parents are a team. Plan your strategy for the interview as a team. Discuss ahead of time what questions you want to have answered by the time the interview is over. Make sure every "team member" has the same questions written down and in front of them during the interview. This way if one person forgets to ask a question, the other one can ask. Also: put all cellphones away and turn off all distractions. You need to stay focused.

Keep score: Write the agent's answers down. This way you won't forget what was said when you discuss them later. Plus, anytime notes are being taken during a meeting, it makes the other person more accountable for his answers.

Play your position: Players and parents can gain a feeling of confidence and control by learning some simple yet effective body language positions and techniques. Keep your head up, shoulders back and engage the agent with a firm handshake. During the introduction, when listening to answers or when you are asking questions maintain eye contact. Keeping your feet flat on the floor, whether you are sitting or standing, helps you feel stable and strong.

Watch for signals: Many agents are both talented and trustworthy. Some are not. By staying alert and noticing signals, you can begin to distinguish one from the other. Notice the agent's handshake. Is it weak or overly aggressive? Do they look you directly in the eyes when you ask a question? Or do they glance away and avoid you? When you ask a direct question, is it answered with facts and details or do they dance all around with the answer?

Focus on results: Your questions are important. Equally important are the answers you will hear. When you have specific and detailed answers, you can make better decisions. So how do you get the details you need? You ask another question! Trustworthy agents will be happy to ensure you have all the answers you need. By writing down the following six open-ended questions and keeping them nearby during the interview, you will get much more than yes or no answers.

1. Can you explain more about that?
2. What exactly does that mean?
3. What is the value or benefit of that?
4. What is the exact process for that?
5. If that did happen, what will happen next?
6. Can you give me an example of that?

WIN: The agent interview process is an important step toward your successful NFL career. By using these guidelines and techniques, you can minimize your stress and maximize your results.

COUNTING THE COST

I regularly have conversations with my subscribers, many of whom are agents. One of these conversations with an agent from a Top-10 firm led to a discussion of the cost of recruiting. Though you, as a parent, won't have to shoulder these costs, I thought it might interest you to know a little more about the economics of the game.

Big budgets: I'm always getting asked by new agents how much money they need to recruit a player. Well, based on that conversation, the figure my friend's firm uses for budgeting is $35,000/player after the signing. This firm doesn't cheat, but I'm still presuming the recruiting costs per player (which probably involve at least 2-3 visits each with probably 2-3 representatives) are around $3,000-$5,000 after you consider plane flights, hotel stays, meals and rental cars. This agency recruits players who range anywhere from 1-50 in the draft (from the first pick in the draft to about midway through the second round). So, basically what I took from that is that if you want to recruit a first-rounder, the baseline is a commitment of about $40,000 to get you to draft day.

It could be worse: I should mention two other related issues. My friend's agency doesn't pay signing bonuses or stipends, which typically run in the five figures. New agents with limited client lists often must figure signing bonuses, even small ones, into the cost, just as a sweetener to get a player to consider them. That number could range into the tens of thousands, but let's just say $10,000, for a grand total of $50,000/player. The other thing my friend added is that if a prospect falls to the third round, the $35,000 becomes a break-even figure. A player has to go in the first two rounds just to turn a profit. Now, a first-rounder in December is just a bad combine, a failed drug test, an arrest or a pulled hamstring on pro day away from the third round (or worse) in April. There are no guarantees in this business, except that bills will come due and you better pay them.

Surcharge: There's one other consideration. Agents who don't have a client list ranging around 20-30 active players have very little shot of signing a player in the top 100. They also must spend, I would estimate, 100 hours on the phone with the player and/or his parents. These are the non-money costs of recruiting.

These costs are not borne by the player or his parents, obviously, but I hope you find it insightful as it pertains to your son's place in the football world.

A COUPLE LAST TIPS

Let's close this chapter with a few final thoughts.

Don't delay: One year, I worked with the parents of a young man who played for a small FBS school. He had had some success on the field and was a solid college player, but he didn't get a lot of attention from agents, so I sent several possible agents his way. I thought we had some agents who would be a great fit, but he delayed in signing. I guess he didn't find that one perfect fit, the one guy whom he felt would represent him perfectly. He continued to deliberate, then wound up having some off-the-field complications that further clouded his life. Ultimately, he never signed. For a player like this, who needed someone to be out lobbying for him, he signed his own death warrant by waiting too long. It's one thing if you're slated to be a first-rounder and ESPN is talking about you every day, but if you're just hoping to go to an NFL camp, I recommend strongly that you make the best decision you can make, pray about it, then go for it.

Training is important but not critical: I think one reason the young man didn't hire an agent is because he couldn't find one who would send him to a big-time training facility. Don't make the same mistake. Look, I know your son has probably heard stories from ex-teammates about the awesome places they went to work out for their pro day or whatever, and maybe they bragged about laying on the beach in January and posted it on Instagram and Twitter, but get past that. Don't sulk and feel sorry for yourself. Get to work. You can do this, but only if you hit it hard, no matter where it is you train. A paid six-week vacation is no substitute for playing in the NFL.

Chapter 5
Interviews With Former Agents

One way to get unabridged truth on a difficult subject is to ask someone with nothing to lose. With that in mind, we interviewed a series of former ITL clients who were once NFLPA-licensed contract advisors to get a nothing-but-the-facts look at football representation, contracts and otherwise. What we got were clear and insightful observations from people who once risked their time, money and sanity on the business.

ITL EXIT INTERVIEW: ROB JEMERSON

A little about Rob, in his own words: "I started in the business because I had a good friend who played wide receiver at James Madison University. When I first met up with him, he had been playing Arena (football), and he had to make the calls himself and didn't have anyone advocating on his behalf. One thing I learned quickly was that if you are going to try to help, you have to follow all the various state regulations, and that's if it's NFLPA or NBPA or MLB or whatever. The states just want their money, and I decided if I was going to make that investment, I had to make it at the level that I got some compensation. So, the first thing I learned is that you can't help people without it costing you money. I went the CFL and NFL route to get fully certified, and from there I registered in every state where I was going to recruit. At the height of my work, and I only did it two years, I had two guys on practice squads. One was a linebacker with the Packers, and one was a Bears tight end. Neither played a regular season game and one is playing Arena now (2012), and one is out of the league."

If you had a son eligible for the NFL draft, what one piece of advice would you give him regarding agent selection?: "(Measure the) liquidity of the agent and (the agent's) character and integrity. I say liquidity because we're seeing now a lot of agents out there who don't have the financial wherewithal to really provide the level of assistance that you need. As a father, I would want to make sure I didn't enter any agreements that would jeopardize his financial well-being. I wouldn't let him sign a deal that wouldn't cover his training expenses. The other part is, it takes a very strong financial commitment to put together the (necessary pre-draft services). And you want character and integrity so it's someone you can trust."

What's the one thing you wish you'd known before you became an agent?: "That the NFLPA is selective in how it enforces the rules and who it enforces the rules against, and even that the NFLPA would make recommendations about who they feel is a qualified agent (to draft prospects). Absolutely. I had a (draft prospect) who called the (NFLPA) and they indicated they thought (a well-known but notorious contract advisor) would be a good person to talk to. That happened. It might be one individual, but you know when the NFLPA has these (pre-combine instructional) caucuses with a few agents, they aren't asking unestablished agents."

ITL EXIT INTERVIEW: MANVEL TRICE

A little about Manvel, in his own words: "I started practicing law in 2001 and became certified with the NFLPA in 2008. I played college basketball for Division II Saginaw Valley State and have played multiple sports for most of my life. In 2006, a colleague of mine and I analyzed how many young men and women, who are natives to Saginaw, went on to play college sports and eventually played at the professional level. We could only think of one or two active sports agents in or from the Saginaw area, so we did our due diligence and devised a plan to break into the industry. After certifying with the NFLPA, I was able to sign my first client, **Charleston Hughes** (who played for the CFL's Calgary franchise and led the CFL in sacks twice), within six months. I signed him with the CFL two months after he signed with me. After playing his first year in the CFL, I was able to set up a number of workouts with NFL teams . . . but this task was made conveniently easy because Hughes, as a rookie, led the CFL in tackles for loss. I negotiated a three-year contract with the Eagles. I began recruiting even more diligently and decided I would have the most success recruiting Division II athletes in Michigan, especially with Hughes having come from Northwood University. I recruited Wayne State and my backyard college, Saginaw Valley, very heavily because I heard about two outstanding football players in (former NFL RB) **Joique Bell** and (former NFL DT) **Robert Callaway**. I attended several of their football games, met with their coaches and athletic directors, introduced myself to their families, and showed up to as many places as I thought they would be. This diligence (paid) off and the geographical proximity to them gave me a leg up on the competition. They both (signed) with me . . . and Joique was a huge blessing because he was . . . one of the top backs (in) the college ranks, who would go on to be invited to the Senior Bowl and the NFL Combine. The whole process was intimidating, but not too big for me or for my client, and I could now smell success, because within two years of being in the business I was able to sign three players to NFL contracts. I even picked up some guys that would never sign an NFL contract, but that experience talking to scouts, personnel, and GMs was unparalleled."

If you had a son eligible for the NFL draft, what one piece of advice would you give him regarding agent selection?: "Find an agent that is going to work hard for you and treat you like you are his or her No. 1 client. Don't go for the most reputable agent. Don't be bamboozled by the agent with the most clients. Don't be led astray by the agent that has negotiated the most money for his clients. Find someone who is going to stand by you through the thick and the thin and make him or her your guy or gal, because loyalty is hard to find in any profession. Don't get me wrong – they have to be competent, they have to be sharp, and they have to be hungry, but they don't have to fit the prototype of most agents, which have led many athletes to a nightmare of financial ruin and missed opportunities."

What's the one thing you wish you'd known before you became an agent?: "The different agent resources available, such as Inside The League, to young agents. I believe there are some mistakes I would not have made early on in my career had I known about such resources. There are some individuals that I would have made a part of my team of advisors had I known about the myriad resources and services available."

ITL EXIT INTERVIEW: NATE HABER

A little about Nate, in his own words: "When I was in law school in the summer of 2007, I met a guy in Cleveland, Andy Simms of PlayersRep (now Young Money APAA) Sports, and he was an agent, and I knew that that was something I always wanted to do, was become an agent. When I met him, I basically just wouldn't let him out of my sight, and I stayed on him and did work with him that summer running a golf outing. I was just trying to show him how hungry I was. And long story short, he taught me about the business. So in the fall of '07, going into the spring of '08, he introduced me to some players. I met with him, and I shadowed him in recruiting, and then in the summer going into '08, I got registered with the NFLPA, and was officially certified, and I joined him full time. We went out and did recruiting together, and in my first year wound up with four picks: two seconds, a third and a sixth. We signed Boston College DT **Ron Brace** and Connecticut DE **Cody Brown,** and then **Bradley Fletcher** out of Iowa and **Brandon Myers** also out of Iowa, and it was a tremendous start. The year after that we had a first-rounder and six other draft picks that year, and so I was just helping him grow the business. The following year we had a few more, and we were going after some new schools, and landing some players. And then in January of 2011 after recruiting ended, I was at a point in my life where I kind of had experienced the business. But after recruiting season was over, I went to him and said, it's time for me to embark on a new path. We have a family company and a family manufacturing business, and then was the right time to do that. It was an emotional decision, but it was a soft landing, so to speak, and then I phased out."

If you had a son eligible for the NFL draft, what one piece of advice would you give him regarding agent selection?: "I would tell him to first and foremost keep it as simple as possible, meaning, have family members help you in the process, someone you trust, and someone who's educated and has a good head on his shoulders, and keep it simple. Don't allow 10, 15, 20 agencies to come into your living room. It gets too muddy. Find former teammates and friends, and have your family make phone calls and do research, and keep it to five that have clients, with a good history and reputation, and once you have those five or six, you know you can't go wrong, and then go with who you trust and feel comfortable with, and someone you feel you could talk to more about football, but also life. For me, that would be it."

What's the one thing you wish you'd known before you became an agent?: "The one thing I would say I wanted to know is that you don't always have as much control as you wished that you would. For a business, this is your livelihood, and there are so many things that are outside your control. It could be players taking gifts from somebody else, or a player's family member is getting a benefit that comes in last minute, or that a guy gets hurt or that he makes a bad decision off the field. Or you've done great work to rehabilitate a player's image, but the scouts have him red-flagged. So if you're in a business where you like to have control of your livelihood, it's a tough business."

ITL EXIT INTERVIEW: MAX HANNEMANN

A little about Max, in his own words: "I was in law school, from 2000-2003, at the University of Hawaii, and one of my best friends at that time was Itula Mili, who was a 10-year veteran of Seahawks, a tight end. We were like best buds, and he told me I should get into the agent game, and I would be a good fit as an agent, and I was getting my law degree which would help solidify negotiating contracts. I passed the bar, then took the agent exam in '04, in July. At the time, you just had to have a college degree, and I was fortunate enough to pass, and then right away I was able to sign Itula. He was not happy with his agent, and he had lost big money due to an agent mistake. So Itula was first and one of my best clients, and right away I was able to sign him to a four-year, $6 million contract, and that was a great experience, and it didn't feel like work to me. I focused on Polynesian players. I'm from Hawaii, and my father is Samoan, and among Polynesians, everybody knows everybody. So because of that, I was able to get my foot in the door to many households. My recruiting was focused on Hawaii and the West Coast; that was my main focus. It's a disadvantage being out here (in Hawaii), because out of sight, out of mind. You're behind the eight-ball with any player you're recruiting at USC or UCLA, because Southern California is like the agent capital of the world. So I did sign some non-Polynesian players, but my main focus was Polynesian players. (Southern Cal OG) **Deuce Lutui** was my highest pick ever, and that also helped. I also signed (Rutgers center) **Cameron Stephenson** out of Rutgers, a real good kid, and (Hawaii FB) **Reagan Mauia,** but there came a time I knew I had to move to the mainland if I really wanted to take my game to the next level. I got a wife and two kids and obviously have to pay the bills and love Hawaii. (But) as each year passed on, it just became such a dirty business."

If you had a son eligible for the NFL draft, what one piece of advice would you give him regarding agent selection?: "My brother, his son was drafted by the Cubs in baseball. He was the first or second pick in the third round, and the advice I gave him was to select someone that you can totally trust. That was the point I always made on the recruiting trail. You gotta hire someone you can totally trust. You need someone that's not going to sugarcoat everything, and you've got to know he's working hard for you, finding avenues for you."

What's the one thing you wish you'd known before you became an agent?: "I guess I was somewhat naïve. I truly thought I could be very successful at being an agent without breaking the rules, and that's very hard to do. You have not only the players to take care of, but also their families. I had a father tell me at the Senior Bowl, who said (his son was undecided about agents), 'Hey Max, I just had an agent give me a fat envelope of cash, what you got for me?' I just said, 'I'm good.' And you hear the sad stories (from parents and family members) about not being able to pay the bills. It's crazy. They're looking for an agent to be their bank, and I couldn't compete. I didn't come from a family of big rich people. I guess I didn't know about the cheating that was out there; a lot more than I expected. And the lies, a lot of lies and unfulfilled promises."

Chapter 6
All-Star Games

There are dozens of questions associated with the all-star process, and plenty at stake for those who don't make the right moves, act promptly, etc. It's much better to handle these issues in early November than in late December or even early January, when it's far too late.

Competition: Whenever I'm talking to parents concerned about their sons' place in the process, it reminds me of January 2007. I was working on my first-ever game in Houston, the **Inta Juice North-South All-Star Classic**. It was pretty heady stuff for me back then, as I'd just launched ITL a few years beforehand and I was already playing a central role in filling the rosters of a game that real NFL scouts would attend. It was a fun fall and winter. Part of what made it fun was that there were two games we were competing against for talent, one in Las Vegas and one in El Paso.

Dispatches: At times, we would hear that others were saying our game wouldn't be played. This infuriated us, but there was little we could do about it. At the same time, we were hearing that the other two games wouldn't be played. We had no way to know if this was true or not, though I'll admit we had a lot of fun considering the possibilities of one or both games falling through. As the weeks progressed, we moved closer and closer to the game itself in early January. We ended up scheduled head to head with two contests that year, the one in Las Vegas and the Hula

Bowl in Honolulu (which, ironically, I would run the following year). On the Friday before our players were scheduled to arrive on Sunday, we started to get credible evidence that the Las Vegas game would, indeed, be canceled. Very soon, the phone calls started pouring into our office line.

Confusion and frustration: We fielded probably 70-80 calls that Friday night from people – mostly parents and the players themselves – who were irate, devastated, shocked, tearful, or all of the above. We wound up taking calls until around 1 a.m., then trudged home, bleary-eyed and empty. But the real calls started the next day. When we arrived at the office that Saturday, we had more than a hundred messages (there's no telling how many actual calls we had received). The voice mails they left were an incredible mess. Callers talked of suing the organizers of the Las Vegas game. They boasted about how scouts were infatuated with their sons. They begged. They pleaded. They threatened. Sometimes, they threatened, then called back, apologizing and begging to be invited. Some offered money. Some parents cried during the message. Some screamed. It was amazing. We wanted to help, but we were trapped. We wound up adding a handful to our roster, but couldn't help many. The others, I guess, tried different options, but I doubt many of them found another game.

This wasn't a life-or-death situation, but it sure felt that way to those parents and those players. And while no one could have predicted that the Vegas game would fail, and so late in the process, it does help to get as educated as possible on these games and really know the ins and outs of things.

HOW DO ALL-STAR GAMES WORK?

Let's answer some of the questions we most often get regarding these games.

What are the costs associated with sending a player to a game? That depends. Up until about 2014, I would have said there are no reputable games that require a player to pay for travel or lodging. Today, however, there are two established games that require its participants to pay for their own travel and/or hotel stay (and I'm even on the board of one of the two games). If your son has been invited to a game, make sure it's been around for more than one year and has former invitees in the league. Spend a little time on the game's website and you should be able to answer those questions. You should also be able to survey agents to find out which games have credibility. Now, as far as who covers those costs, typically it's the agent, but you'll want to make sure that's cleared with any contract advisor your son is considering beforehand.

Does an all-star game get a player drafted? There are some established agencies that don't send players to all-star games unless it's one of the top two games, the Senior Bowl (the No. 1 game) and the Shrine Game (No. 2). You'll want to ask prospective agencies their all-star philosophy. Some agencies' reasoning is that there aren't enough true decision-makers at the lesser games to really move the needle for their clients. Maybe that's true, but these games are still generally considered a huge help to players, especially outside the top 100 slated to go in the draft. A good week can put a late-rounder into the middle rounds, or a projected undrafted free agent into the draft. What's more, if a player's pro day doesn't attract many scouts, at least he's on the radar screen with all the teams that attended the game. Most teams send scouts to all legitimate games. Usually, a game has about a hundred participants, and 60-70 players from even the smallest all-star games wind up on NFL rosters the following summer. Those are good odds.

Does it get a player into the combine? Not really. When I ran the Hula Bowl in 2008, it was the earliest game in the all-star cycle (in early January). One of our QBs, Marshall's **Bernard Morris**, had an excellent week and a great game, and his performance vaulted him into an invitation to Indianapolis in February. These days, however, as more and more juniors leave early for the draft, most seniors are invited well before all-star play begins. The last 100 players invited are almost all juniors, and except for a handful that are invited to the Senior Bowl, they are ineligible for all-star games.

How fluid is the all-star selection process? It's very fluid. *Very, very fluid.* As we've already discussed, the key is identifying the one person with an all-star game who has personnel responsibilities, knowing how to reach him, and building a good relationship with him in a timely manner. As we've mentioned before, it's important to make sure your agent choice has these connections.

GO TIME

Here are a few pointers for making sure your son improves his chances of getting into a postseason showcase.

Behind the scenes: The all-star invitation process is one of the most overlooked parts of the college/pro game. Media and coaches are focused on the week's college games, but the people running all-star games are focused on what's happening in January. It all starts with player selection. Sometimes I think there's a perception that these invites don't go out until the college season is virtually over. Not true. Not long ago, invitees were a closely guarded secret, but today, you can check the websites for the top games to find out who's already confirmed starting in November. By the time the games arrive, it's pretty common knowledge who's going where.

Be your own advocate: Remember that, in most cases, all-star play is not a priority for your coaches. In all my years running games, I can only remember a few instances where a coach for a team really went to bat for his players during the regular season and truly lobbied to get his players into a game. Sometimes after the season the coaches played a role, but by then, it's way harder to make things happen for their players. I remember one time I called a major ACC school in October or November, and the football operations coach I talked to basically said, "What do I care? This isn't my responsibility." I thought that was astonishing but not entirely surprising. This leads us to our next point.

You may have already been invited: I was emailing with an all-star game's personnel director one year, and I asked him how things were going. He indicated that he'd sent out several invites, some to the players directly and some to coaches at the schools, and that "most coaches have said they will be giving (the invitations) to the kids in the coming week." Holding invites for players is not uncommon, and many coaches hold invitations far longer than until after the next game. Many teams see all-star invites as a distraction from the real work of winning football games, and they may be right. However, if you feel your son is a legitimate NFL prospect, once his regular season ends, I'd recommend checking with the team's football operations or pro liaison coach to make sure he's not holding something for him.

A quick (and sad) story: I remember in January of 2007, when we were wrapping up the invitation process for my first game, we suddenly got flooded by calls from TCU players. Their coaches had held their invitations until after the completion of their season, so they hadn't received them until well after the completion of bowl play. We had already replaced all of these kids. It was very tough. How do you avoid having your son left out in the cold? Be respectful and wait until it's appropriate to check with team officials (I suggest after your regular season) about invites. Don't let the TCU case happen to you.

GOING TO BAT

Self-promotion is not instinctual to a lot of athletes, but reaching out to all-star games on your son's behalf is not a terrible idea.

Lobbying is a big part of things: I think there's a perception that everything scouts do – and everything done by people associated with NFL football – is very cut and dried. Many believe that finding the best players is pretty easy, and that future pro football players stick out from the crowd. For a lot of reasons, that's not true, even today, when the Internet allows us to watch football games or players' highlights anywhere, any time. For this reason, reaching out to game organizers is critical. The earlier, the better. Getting in contact with game organizers isn't easy because you have to know who to talk to, but it's still a big part of the game. That's one reason why the agent selection process is so important. Of course . . . .

Parents can lobby for players: Your son doesn't have to wait to sign with an agent to start making his all-star case with game officials. Again, you have to know who to contact, and you can't just fire off emails through the "Contact Us" portal on a game's website and expect real results. It's also helpful if you can point out strengths, like geographical ties to the region where the game is played (think ticket sales), or years of starting at a key position, or playing for an impressive program, or other selling points. Also, if your son played for an FBS school before transferring to a smaller school and starring, point that out as well. One note: Be careful about copying the whole NFL Draft Scout page and just forwarding it. Every time I've run a game, I've gotten dozens of those. It gets irritating. I don't care what the media says about a player. I care what scouts say.

Players can lobby for themselves: I don't think I've ever worked on a game when we didn't take at least one young man who contacted us on his own via email, phone or both. Naturally, we didn't take kids just because they said they wanted to play – we vetted them through scouts first – but it didn't hurt when they expressed an interest in the game. I remember one such player, Michigan State DT **Ogemdi Nwagbuo**, who played for me in the 2008 Hula Bowl. He played six years in the NFL. It's doubtful we would ever have taken him if he hadn't emailed us one day, asking to be considered for the game.

I want to warn you. Next, we're going to talk about some things that might sound self-serving and a little selfish, but they aren't. I want you to act in an honorable way, obviously, but I also want you to maximize your chances of success on the next level. Sometimes that means doing hard things. So, we are going to talk about some actions that may seem counter to your instincts, but trust me, they're points I feel must be made.

An all-star commitment can be broken: If your son gets invited to an all-star game, that's wonderful news, and I encourage him to accept that invitation ASAP. Now, during the course of the season, several games will send out invites, then wait to receive a commitment from the player. That's because most young men are waiting for other games to call, and they don't want to mislead a game. Look, the organizers of games know full well where they stand in the pecking order, and if they're inviting a player, it's because game officials think the players is going to say yes. If a player commits to a game, but in the next couple weeks gets another opportunity, as long as he tells the first game's officials in a timely fashion, he will be released from his commitment with their blessing. If game officials pressure him to keep his commitment, shame on them. If you're not sure what game he should go to, ask a team official or agent. Remember, Senior Bowl is king and all other games are somewhere behind it.

It's (almost) never too late: If you don't hear from a game in October or November and the silence drags into mid-December, it doesn't mean it's all over for your son. It does, however, mean someone – an agent, a parent, a coach, himself -- better start making some noise. That's where it's beneficial to start reaching out to games and asking them where they have him rated. Now, first, he has to be honest with himself. Is he really a legitimate NFL prospect? If your son honestly feels like he is, then communicate with a game's personnel director, or get an agent who'll do it for you.

No strings attached: Let's say your son is in the final stages of agent selection and one of the contenders to sign him calls excitedly to tell him he's being invited to a game. That's great, and I hope he expresses his appreciation, and maybe even gives that agent an edge in the decision-making process. But he shouldn't feel like he owes it to the agent to sign with him. At the end of the day, these games invite players not because of their agent, but because of the interest scouts have in the player. He will be going to a game because of what he's done on the playing field as well as his potential on the next level, and everybody understands that. Year after year, I have agent clients who call me with tales of woe about players they got into games who didn't sign with them. I offer them a shoulder to cry on, but I can't fault the player for seizing an opportunity like that.

ALL-STAR GAME OVERVIEW

Here's a quick look at the various all-star games on the schedule, and where they stand in the pecking order. I should mention that the all-star lineup changes year to year, with several games hanging around a year or two before disappearing. All of these games are played in January.

Senior Bowl (Mobile, Ala.): This is the No. 1 game, hands down, mainly because it maintains a partnership with the NFL which allows two NFL teams to send their entire coaching staffs to coach the teams. The Senior Bowl is the only game that consistently features players who will be drafted in the first round. The Senior Bowl is *the* offseason destination for virtually everyone in the NFL and a good number of college coaches as well, many of whom see the game as a networking event and job fair.

East-West Shrine Game (St. Petersburg, Fla.): This game is generally agreed to be the No. 2 contest even though it hasn't enjoyed nearly the same acclaim and stability of the Senior Bowl. The bulk of Shrine Game participants are drafted in the fourth round and lower, though most years 2-3 players will be selected in the second or third round.

NFLPA Collegiate Bowl (Los Angeles): This game has had its ups and downs but seems poised to move past the Shrine Game in the all-star pecking order. Given that it's located in California, it's historically attracted more players from West Coast schools. The game recently hired former Buffalo Bills GM **Doug Whaley**, which should give it even more momentum.

College Gridiron Showcase (Fort Worth, Texas): The College Gridiron Showcase is unique in that its founders, Jose Jefferson and Craig Redd, had the guts to ask players to cover their own travel costs and, in some cases, hotel costs, as well, when it debuted in 2014. Several years later, the game is a fixture on the all-star game schedule, partially due to Jose and Craig's innovations. By the way, I serve on the board of the CGS.

Tropical Bowl (Daytona Beach, Fla.): Like the CGS, Michael Quartey's game requires its participants to cover their own travel costs and pay a discounted hotel fee. Also, like the CGS, the game has developed a solid following among NFL teams. Quartey, a former agent, really has a heart for helping young men pursue their dreams, and he's seen his game take annual strides since it debuted a few years ago.

THE SHRINE GAME

Let's take a closer look at the top two games on the all-star circuit, the Senior Bowl (No. 1) and the Shrine Game (No. 2). We'll take a look at the Shrine Game first since it's first on the calendar each year.

NFL scouts: One of the biggest concerns of agents is always how many scouts will be attending a game, but no worries here; there will be no shortage of personnel types in South Florida. Most teams will send 3-4 scouts, including their directors of college scouting. There will be a handful of general managers there (usually 4-5). Usually the Buccaneers send their GM because it's practically a home game for them, and maybe the Dolphins and Jaguars.

However, at the end of the day, there are no concerns about the level of NFL interest and the "eyeballs," because they'll be there.

Rain: The weather can be a little unpredictable in South Florida in January. Lately it's warm and a little breezy. Sometimes it rains really hard, and that's unfortunate, because the teams have to hold walk-throughs in the hotel ballroom. Of course, there's nothing anyone can do about that, but if it happens, don't say I didn't warn you. Oh, by the way – the Shrine Game is one of the last games that pays players a stipend for participation, so that should be some consolation if it rains.

Combine invitees: Usually, about two-thirds to three-fourths of the players on the roster will be headed to Indianapolis in February. That number has declined a bit in recent years because so many juniors have chosen to leave early, reducing the number of seniors who get called to Indy. Many scouts I talk to lament the declining talent level at the Shrine Game, but it's nobody's fault. There are just fewer elite players who stick around four years anymore, and the Shrine Game doesn't take juniors.

Agents: Here's one question I always get: what if my son goes to a game without an agent? There's nothing wrong with that, and he won't lose anything if that happens, so he shouldn't feel like there's a big clock on the wall if he just hasn't found someone he's comfortable with. One of the advantages, if he does have an agent, is that he has someone around for questions or other issues (equipment, minor injury, travel) that need attention. It's also not so bad to have an advocate among the scouts roaming the practice field. But at the end of the day, a player's performance on the field is going to speak volumes even if there's not a contract advisor around to promote his work. In 2013, there were nine players who arrived in St. Pete without an agent, which is a really high number. The thing is, your son should prepare to be recruited when he's down there if he lacks representation. That may be a positive, but may be a negative if it becomes a distraction. It's just something you need to know in advance.

The schedule: Because of its history and the reason the game is played (to support the efforts of the Shriners' Hospitals, especially young burn victims), there's more pageantry to the Shrine Game than there is to any other all-star game. However, after the big dinner and the hospital visit on opening weekend, the focus will be on football early in the week. Be prepared for three reasonably high-intensity workouts in full pads (Monday, Tuesday and Wednesday), then two days of going over plays and special teams in shorts and shells (Thursday and Friday). Monday through Wednesday, game organizers mostly leave you alone so scouts can get their individual interviews done, but as you move toward Thursday and Friday, there's more pageantry and fan-oriented events, highlighted by the dinner Friday night.

When should parents come?: This is a very common question. Technically, they can come whenever they want to, though I don't recommend it. I remember two years ago during an all-star game in Montgomery, Ala., one father stood on the sideline at practices all week, watching his son. That man got treated to some of the worst weather I've ever had to endure during a game week, with cold winds, intermittent rain and generally miserable weather. What's more, the conditions made practices very sloppy. Parents who come down early probably won't see that kind of cold weather in South Florida, but they might get torrential rain. They also might be bored when it's not practice time, and players only practice for about an hour-and-a-half each day, anyway. I usually recommend parents come down Thursday night, hang out on Friday, attend the dinner Friday night, then go to the game on Saturday. Early in the week, players need their space to get work done with NFL officials. His agent might also want to take him to dinner. It's better not feeling you have to play host, especially Monday to Wednesday. The Senior Bowl offers a lot more for parents, but we'll dig into that later.

Off the field: St. Petersburg is a resort town, and the team hotel is on an island with sandy beaches right behind the hotel (though it might be a little too cold for a dip). What's more, there are bars and restaurants up and down the main road through town, so it's easy to find a reasonably priced hotel room and a meal. The town is pretty quiet in the winter. The only folks around are business owners who cater to tourists and the mostly elderly who live in Florida year-round. Roll into a bar or restaurant, especially early in the week, and you've pretty much got the place to yourself. As for the players, most evenings they're milling around the lobby waiting to be interviewed by scouts. The Tradewinds, the team hotel, has plenty of space to lounge in the lobby and several TV screens.

THE SENIOR BOWL

As you know by now, the Senior Bowl is the No. 1 game in the all-star landscape. It's a big deal, and rightfully so. In fact, if someone dropped a bomb on Ladd-Peebles stadium during the late morning or midafternoon during the third week in January, it would essentially wipe out the NFL's coaching and scouting staffs. For this reason, you want to be prepared.

The big stage: You may have heard that players will be graded on everything that happens in Mobile, and that's pretty much true. It's not so much that invitees need to be nervous every second they're there or be scared they could get downgraded if they use bad table manners or forget to floss their teeth. But everything attached to football should be done at their *very* best.

Punctuality counts: This goes without saying, but being on time matters. Here's an example. In 2014, a friend of mine in the media had to give two players, Missouri DE **Michael Sam** and Michigan State S **Isaiah Lewis**, a ride to practice after they missed the bus. Sam went in the seventh round and Lewis went undrafted. I have often wondered if the fact they couldn't be punctual for one week of practices had an impact on their draft status. Here's another example. The year I ran the Hula Bowl, in 2008, I had a Bucs scout specifically ask me if we had had any problems with any players that week, from a character standpoint. We had, and I told him about the one kid who had been a constant problem (punctuality was one of his issues). He went undrafted. Maybe it had something to do with our conversation, maybe it didn't. But I know it didn't help.

Optimal conditions: Among the things the Senior Bowl has over other games is the practice field. All practices are held on turf at the game field, Ladd-Peebles Stadium. Shrine Game practices are held on grass at two different schools in St. Petersburg. I've never been to the NFLPA Collegiate Bowl, so I don't know how it runs practices, but other games often require scouts to drive 15-20 minutes to catch workouts. The Senior Bowl gives you an opportunity to work out free of mud or lousy surfaces, and it is just about seven minutes from the team hotel. Those are positives. Players also get access to the Mobile Bay Convention Center, where the league sets up for physicals, meetings, testing and weigh-ins. Access is controlled, of course, so you're not going to have any weirdos walking through, but otherwise, it's a great place to hold things. The hospitality is great, too. The people at the Senior Bowl really pride themselves on welcoming players and it shows. It's a good time.

The team hotel: At the Senior Bowl, every player and almost every NFL scout, coach and administrator will be housed in the Renaissance Mobile Riverview Plaza Hotel. It's a very nice place, and it's attached to the city's convention center, where a lot of Senior Bowl events (weigh-ins, medical reviews, press events) will take place. The hotel is completely booked out by the NFL all week, so parents, friends, coaches, or anyone else not employed by the league or an NFL team will not be able to stay there. Of course, that doesn't mean they can't spend a lot of time in the hotel's lobby, bar, restaurant, or mezzanine level, where most players and scouts hang out during the week.

Arrival of guests: One question you might have is, when is a good time for parents, friends, or other visitors to arrive? I usually recommend they come in Thursday night or sometime on Friday. If they arrive around late afternoon on Thursday, they can get in, register with their hotel, get their credentials, have dinner that evening, visit with the players in a relaxed setting, then catch practices the next day before going to the game on Saturday. The "business" of the Senior Bowl takes place early in the week, especially the first three days, which is when players are practicing in pads and scouts are most interested in workouts.

Off-the-field evaluation: The early part of the week is also the time when weigh-ins are conducted – this is probably the most-watched, most popular event of the week – and it's when scouts are working hard to get all their interviews done with the players they've come to see. On Mondays, especially, it's not unusual to see scouts rushing around the mezzanine level, catching young men and escorting them to the nearest table for a quick question-and-answer session. Many scouts also hand out questionnaires as the players come out of weigh-ins. It's all part of the evaluation process.

SOME THINGS TO REMEMBER

I want to touch on a few topics I often see at all-star games that players need to be aware of, especially when things don't go their way.

Conditions: When it's rainy, it can make for really lousy conditions in workouts. Some years, I lose count of the drops, bobbles, fumbled snaps and other mishandled balls, especially early in the week. What's more, receivers can't come out of their breaks and linemen can't hold their positions in drills because they simply can't get traction. It can be a sloppy mess for both teams, and this leads to a lot of frustration on the part of players as well as scouts.

Bad plays: Guess what? Every receiver is going to miss a catch. Linemen will allow penetration, and maybe even a sack. Defensive players will get driven backward. Passers will make bad throws. Tacklers will slip and miss. It happens.

Awkward situations: I've been told by scouts that even if players don't work out at the combine in Indianapolis, it's still a great event because it allows teams to sit down with players and interview them. To some degree, the same is true of all-star games. This is why scouts leave on Wednesday and sometimes even Tuesday: they've gotten their interviews done, so it's time to go home. It's possible a player will get asked a question that he wasn't prepared for. He might have a situation he can't explain. It happens. He just needs to be as honest as possible and make it clear that life is a learning process, and that he won't make the same mistake twice.

Speaking of awkward situations, parents should advise their sons to be honest about their personal lives as well. For example, are there girlfriend issues that need to be addressed? It's better to be upfront about such matters before they come to the fore in the news media. Also, it may be good to warn your sons about female attention if and when they get drafted. Forewarned is forearmed.

Agent/training situations: A player may be solicited by people during an all-star week. It might be an agent who won't take no for an answer. It might be a trainer who's a pest. It might be a financial planner insisting that he'd like to schedule a meeting. Make sure your son does his best to keep them at arm's length.

The bottom line: All of the above situations are negatives, but don't panic. I've been going to all-star games for close to two decades, and I've seen some pretty poor performances. Often, they were given by players who went on to lengthy, successful NFL careers. No matter if the conditions are lousy, your son's performance is bad, or he gets rattled by an off-the-field situation, he shouldn't let it kill his confidence.

Chapter 7
Combine Prep

There has been no greater change in the NFL draft over the last 15 years than the rise of combine preparation facilities and the belief that training for pro days should be completed not at players' schools, but at specialized locations where the focus is on strength and speed. Let's cover the basics of this practice.

When does training take place?: Traditionally, combine prep starts the first full week of January and continues for six to eight weeks, depending on the date of the combine and/or a player's pro day. Most facilities have a morning and afternoon session of about an hour to two hours each, and have training Monday through Friday, though this varies; some take Wednesdays off and have a Saturday morning session, or take the weekends completely off. Trainees usually eat a diet and consume supplements provided by nutritionists at the facility, and everything that goes in their mouths is aimed at providing whatever the player needs (weight loss, weight gain, etc.) to hone their bodies.

Combine vs. pro day training: These days, most facilities offer two packages. The combine prep package is for your upper-echelon players, and starts the first week of January, then runs through February. If participants don't actually get a combine invite – invitations aren't all sent out until well into January – they usually train through their pro day sometime in March. Combine prep packages almost always include food and supplements, while those are a la carte additions for pro day packages. Typically, combine prep packages are at least double what a pro day package costs.

What happens after the combine or pro day?: Most trainers will allow their clients to return and train between the combine and/or their pro day date for as much as they want. The problem is that if the player doesn't have lodging near the gym, someone needs to pay for it. That can be a hard sell to an agent who's already paid for eight weeks of training, lodging and food.

Where does it take place?: As combine prep has become more popular, more and more gyms are offering it (and getting good at it). Most of the top trainers are located in the Sun Belt, and as top players have become accustomed to spending their winters training in a sunny, tropical climate, the bigger agencies most often send their clients to South Florida. While there are also premier facilities in Arizona, Texas and California, South Florida has become synonymous with combine prep, and many top trainers have moved to the Sunshine State to stay relevant in the business. Of course, there's a premium to be paid for training in Florida in deluxe accommodations, so some agents and/or players look to other locations to get great training at more competitive prices. Speaking of accommodations, most players sleep at a nearby extended-stay hotel or an apartment complex where the trainer has a special rate, and this cost is folded into the cost of the training package. Usually a player has at least one roommate, though bigger-name players sometimes demand their own rooms from agents eager to satisfy every need during the recruiting process. The cost of residency has overtaken the actual cost of training in some areas, especially in South Florida where short-term housing is pretty expensive.

The total training package: So, what's included in the cost of eight weeks of training? Usually the agent or player and his family are responsible for the cost of travel to and from the facility. Once there, the facility provides training, lodging and, most often, three meals a day for five days per week. Most trainers take on a class of 12-15 athletes (usually 20 or less), and while they all get very invested in their athletes and their training, there are no guarantees that results will be achieved. At the end of the day, every player gets out of the training what he puts into it. The cost of a training package can be anywhere from a per-week basis of around $100, with no meals or lodging provided, to $25,000 or more for the entire term, usually with some bells and whistles included. The cost and size of the package usually depends on how highly the player is rated going into the draft.

Position-specific training: One of the more recent trends in the business is to offer specialists (usually ex-NFL players) who work one on one with combine trainees honing their skills. In fact, in the fall of 2013, one of the leaders in combine preparation, Exos (formerly Athletes Performance), announced that it had hired Hall of Fame QB **Warren Moon** to do just that for the passers in its 2014 class. This is one of the value-adds that many services are offering, but there are a number of other bells and whistles when it comes to combine prep.

Bells and whistles: While the main thrust of the time spent training is focused on reducing a player's 40 time and other drills while gaining strength and explosion, there are a number of extras that can also be provided. Some locations provide massages as a basic part of the package, while others provide them a la carte. Rehabilitation services are also a critical part of the package for some facilities, and some keep physical therapists and/or orthopedists on staff full time to attend to injured players. Another common add-on is interview training provided by ex-NFL scouts or administrators; there's even one former NFL GM who provides such training full time at a rather expensive rate. His specialty is covering the questions teams commonly ask at the combine and on team visits, especially for players slated to go in the first three rounds and/or those who have background issues that may create trouble. We at Inside the League have been offering this service for the better part of 10 years with selected agencies. Interview training has become so common that some see it as a necessary part of the process; different facilities provide their own spin on this practice, bringing in a local team official, or using a sports psychologist, or perhaps using an ex-actor – all with the aim of training athletes to be calm in front of the lights and cameras.

Who gets training?: More and more, players eligible for the coming draft see combine prep as a right or an entitlement, and expect their agents to pay for it. As a rule of thumb, all non-kickers invited to the combine (slightly more than 300 players) will probably train somewhere other than their school. After that, it kind of varies. Some players will find agents with open checkbooks who see training as part of the process, and these agents might give their clients pretty of free rein about deciding where they'll train. Such agents are becoming rare, however, as combine prep costs rise and some question its benefits over training at school. Agents who are recently certified are most likely to be the ones who offer to cover combine prep for virtually anyone they sign. This has become a classic mistake, as many athletes pursue an agent who offers all-expenses-paid training over one who may offer a less-enticing training package, but who is willing to work hard, be responsive, maintain a good communication level and overall do the things a good agent does.

As we've mentioned previously, the rise of combine prep facilities is the biggest change in the draft business in the last decade. Of course, these things must be funded somehow, so let's spend some time on the economics. We'll break it down by prospect level.

Combine invitees: If your son is a combine invitee, you can find an agent to pay for his training. He may not get to train at Bommarito Performance (Miami), XPE Sports (Fort Lauderdale), Exos (formerly Athletes Performance, with locations across the country), TEST Football Academy (New Jersey), Parabolic Performance & Rehab (New Jersey), California Strength (Bay Area), EFT Sports Performance (Chicago) or one of the other top services in the business, but he'll get his training paid for somewhere. He may also not get his first choice agent-wise, and you both might have to make a business decision based on how much he values training somewhere other than his school, but he'll probably find training.

Starter at FBS school: If your son started his senior season and played for a successful Division I-A school, he will have a chance to have his training paid for. Of course, there are several variables. If he played an impact position

(DE, LT, QB, CB, etc.); played at a BCS school; started multiple years; arrived at his school as a highly touted recruit; or has extraordinary physical skills (4.3 40, or an Olympic background), he has a better chance of getting his training covered. If he was a one-year starter; has a background of arrests; played a low-impact position (OG, box safety, PK, PT, etc.); or lacks NFL dimensions and/or speed for his position, chances are you'll struggle to find someone to pay.

The training rider: Either way, a good agent will cover himself by asking a player to sign a training rider. This rider will state that all training fees are covered as long as he doesn't fire the agent before signing an NFL deal. You'll find some agents that might not ask for your son to sign such a rider, but be careful there, because either that agent is so desperate to sign him that he's probably in over his head, or he's so lacking in knowledge of how the industry works that he'll be liable to make a costly mistake down the line that could have a major impact on you and your son. Of course, before your son signs a rider, he should realize that it will make it much tougher to fire that agent in most circumstances. If you dump your contract advisor in March, your son will be preparing for his pro day while simultaneously trying to find a new agent willing to cover training costs. If your son is projected to go in the first three rounds, that's no problem, but if not, it's going to be a lot more difficult. Training riders may be tricky, and it may feel like they inhibit your freedom, but it's the only way agents can protect themselves and their investments.

Training at school: If your son played at a BCS school, or at nearly any FBS school in the era of big-money athletics, he probably have access to sufficient facilities and coaches to train for his pro day. As recently as 10 years ago, virtually all training was conducted this way. Of course, back then, pro days and the combine weren't nearly as critical as they are now, but it still gives you some idea of the players who made it to the next level without concierge-level pre-draft training. I even once had a trainer who got out of the business because he was convinced that combine training did nothing that an athlete couldn't do on his own given proper rest, nutrition, disciplined training and simply letting his body heal. I don't necessarily subscribe to that belief, but the bottom line is that if your son winds up training at school, he isn't locked out of the NFL. Just look at all the players who trained at school and still wound up in the first round (examples include Alabama's **Amari Cooper** and Iowa's **Brandon Scherff** in 2015, Texas A&M's **Myles Garrett** in 2017 and Alabama's **Calvin Ridley** in 2018). All of them were selected in the top 32 without having the benefit of a tony, expensive combine prep facility. It *can* be done.

Paying for training: If your son is insistent on training somewhere other than at school, and the agents you talk to aren't offering it, it's time to have a frank discussion with them – and yourself. It's important to really have a sense of where your son fits into the draft, and it may be time to find a facility that's within driving distance of your home or school and that offers competent training but perhaps without the bells and whistles. There are dozens of no-frills gyms out there that can offer affordable training, and we regularly recommend them to parents, players and agents when there's a need. Bottom line, if combine training is something that's critical to your son, you may have to work out a split with an agent, maybe offering to go 50-50 or some other ratio. Many agents, especially those with limited client lists, may be willing to make this arrangement, and it's becoming more and more common. I can't tell you how many times I've heard of players or their parents making ill-conceived ultimatums and pricing themselves out of representation.

A case study: Here's what *not* to do. One year, I was attending an all-star game in Allen, Texas, and I told one of my agent clients (who was newly certified) which players were not yet signed. He eagerly approached one such player, a true long shot, about signing him, and was referred to his father, who advised my client that he "had a background in sports marketing." What that meant is that the father wanted to play big shot. Well, he talked his son right out of representation, and of course, the young man went undrafted and didn't even receive a camp invite. Meanwhile, the agent was so discouraged that he called me about a week later and told me he was getting out of the business. Sad but true.

Specialists: Punters, kickers and long-snappers may get timed in the 40, L Drill (the 3-cone agility / balance drill), short shuttle, etc., because they show up at a pro day and scouts may be afraid not to. However, their speed and agility are not central to their jobs. For that reason, typically they either work out on their own at school or, in some cases, go to specialized locations (usually in the Southwest or West Coast) where they receive training from ex-NFL position coaches or former kickers. In either case, there is a lot less money typically spent on them because they make so much less and their jobs are usually so tenuous anyway.

Quarterbacks: Passers are on the other end of the spectrum. Usually, they demand at least one week of one-on-one training. The truly elite go through their own eight-week regimen, sometimes at separate training facilities; in fact, the "celebrity quarterback trainer" has become a cottage industry and a subset of the combine prep industry these days. The main thrust of these QB trainers has become setting up "the script." As pro days and the draft process have become more and more publicized and hype-filled, you're starting to see top-rated quarterbacks' pro days broadcast nationally. That's where these trainers, often half-promoter, half-guru, come in. The more polished ones speak in sound bites for the camera, create buzz with scouts, then stand studiously behind their prodigies during a drill that has been practiced for weeks (and, of course, takes place without a pass rush). Afterward, the guru points out to the media how his pupil only threw one incomplete pass, or none, or whatever.

Mostly hype: If it sounds like I'm poking fun at this process, I am (a little). I was talking to a veteran NFL and college QB coach about ex-Texas passer **Chris Simms** several years ago, and I'll never forget one thing he told me. He said that, in order to fix a flaw so it won't be repeated under duress, it takes about 10,000 throws done correctly. Think about that. It would take 500 straight days of training, at 200 throws per day, to see real results for a quarterback who side-arms the ball, has a hitch in his delivery, winds up before releasing the ball, or whatever. My point is that these high-level trainers are good for burnishing a few things, solidifying footwork, getting a passer to hold the ball higher, or helping them on the chalkboard, but they can't change in eight weeks what a kid has been doing over his career. At the end of the day, if your son is a quarterback, don't worry too much if he doesn't have the attention of one of the big-name specialists. There's a lot of "show" in their game anyway. No one's going to turn a small-school backup into John Elway.

One other note: Your son probably got all, or some, of his college paid for via scholarship. Many parents see this as a reason to spend $25,000-$30,000 at a premier combine prep location. I don't recommend this. If your son has "got it," some agent will recognize this and cover your son's training costs. If not, no trainer can turn him from a marginal prospect into a draftable one. I recommend capping any training you pay for at $10,000, and even then, only if you can easily afford it. Think of training as polishing a stone, not turning it into a gem.

TRAINING DECISIONS

Combine prep is a big part of the pre-draft process, and your son may have been approached by trainers and others who've discussed different facets of workouts and drills. As you both weigh a training location, it's important to know what to look for as well as keeping focus on what's important. With that in mind, we spoke to Kevin Dunn, who's got more than two decades in combine prep as the owner of TEST Football Academy in Martinsville, N.J.

Every rep counts: "The pre-draft process is one that has proven to potentially elevate draft stock as well as cost others millions due to a lack of preparation. It is a true display of maturity in a young man to show up fully ready and prepared with zero excuses, looking forward to confidently attacking each drill. This confidence is showcased on the field because he knows all the answers to the TEST before he arrives."

Results matter: "You're looking for guys that have a track record, both with rookies and veterans who return after training before the draft. The next draft class (2019) will mark our 20-year anniversary working with athletes, with more than 250 athletes delivered to professional football and 61 current players spread across 25 NFL teams."

Is everything there?: "Advanced facilities have invested in things like Keiser air-based pneumatic technology, Power Plate vibration technology, MyZone heart rate and calorie tracking, video analysis software, Apple TV-compatible 60-inch flat screens and a well-designed (application) to track every workout. The facility should also be clean, well-organized and functional."

Environment matters: "This is not a paid vacation. The weather in Florida or California in January and February is hard to beat. Maybe you can handle that, maybe you can't. You're planning for the most critical final exam of your life. Selecting the site where you train in is paramount to your success. When it's time to study, you're maybe better off going to the library. Welcome to Jersey in January and February. It's like *Rocky IV*."

Medicals matter: "A third of the NFL Combine is medical. Most of the first day in Indianapolis is spent getting MRIs, X-rays, blood work, drug testing, etc., and even if you don't go to the combine, no team will draft you without an extensive physical and medical records check.

Upon arrival at TEST, we dedicate an entire day to a medical review and evaluation from an orthopedic physician, physical therapist, chiropractor, nutritionist, meal prep service, sport psychologist and our director of football operations. Each of these professionals has been on our team for many years helping our athletes to maximize the grueling physical and mental process these young men are exposed to."

Look for personal attention: "Personal attention and motivation are critical for the success of your performance. Football is a team sport, and teammates motivate one another, but the size of the group must be considered. Too small a group and it will lack the tangible benefits of a 'team.' Equally, too large a group and the athlete can get lost. The ratio that we have seen to be most beneficial has been one coach to six athletes. Confirm the facility that makes this claim does not count an unpaid intern as a coach. This ratio allows enough rest between sets, provides motivation in small groups, and allows us to maximize the film review immediately after the rep."

INTERVIEW SKILLS

Probably the most asked-for a la carte service is interview skills training. It's one of the most popular additions to combine prep facilities in the last five years, and some schools even try to require interview skills training as a condition of signing players. But is such training really necessary?

Who needs training?: This is a two-part answer. First, is your son going to the combine? If he is, he probably needs some form of instruction. If he's not, he probably doesn't, for a couple reasons. If he's already played in an all-star game, he's already been interviewed by scouts anyway, so he's less likely to be interviewed again at his pro day. If he didn't play in an all-star game, chances are teams will be more focused on his on-field performance at his pro day, and interviews are pretty secondary.

Who doesn't need training?: Even if your son is headed to Indianapolis for the NFL Combine, I wouldn't worry too much about interview training if (a) he doesn't have any skeletons in his closet and (b) he is well-spoken and did well in school. He's likely training somewhere that includes interview skills instruction, but if not, and you feel confident he doesn't have any major off-the-field issues, don't worry about this too much.

Please note: If you know your son has a serious red flag – he was kicked off the team, has multiple arrests, transferred multiple times, his head coach is working against him –his agent probably needs to have a serious talk with him. He needs to be grilled on the issues facing him to see how he handles them. If the NFL is a realistic for your son, interview skills training may be worth considering if he's got things in his background that are a concern. At some point, if he's a legitimate NFL possibility, he's going to get questioned at length by NFL scouts. He's going to need to handle that correctly. Even if he performs well at his pro day or at a private workout, he'll get passed over if he creates doubt in the minds of NFL teams. There are always "safer" possibilities with similarly talented players. We have worked with players who went into January rated as second-round talents who went undrafted because of a character issue.

What does it cost?: Each winter, we contract with various agents to send a former NFL GM to work with their respective draft prospects. Among those we've used in the past are **Ray Farmer** (now with the Rams), **Phil Emery** (now with the Falcons), **Jerry Angelo** (who's retired) and **Jeff Ireland** (now with the Saints). Depending on how much time our guy spends with a player, his draft projection, and where he's training, it can cost from a couple hundred dollars to a thousand or more per player. There are also some players we handle in a group setting; their costs are much lower, of course. There are interview specialists who charge closer to $2,000 per player after travel and lodging are figured in, and most of them only want to work with players rated in the first three rounds. Some agents will provide their own interview prep, or will try to recruit only players who are high character and don't have the kind of background that warrants spending extra money to handle. You'll also find the odd retired scout who lives near a training facility and is the "in-house" option for all their trainees. Bottom line, you can pay lots of different prices depending on the level of service and the perceived needs of the player. Rely on your son's agent and what you know about your son's history before any decisions are made. Not every player needs special attention.

TAKING STOCK

February is a tough month. Not much is happening, and it becomes a waiting game. There are a few things to remember.

Forget about January: This is especially true if your son didn't get an all-star invite. Every year, I have numerous conversations with parents from November through January as they wait for their sons to get an all-star call that never comes. This is particularly vexing for me. Every year, I attend virtually every all-star game, and I can see that the best players aren't always on the field at various positions. This takes place even though, at times, I lobby game organizers to take certain players. Ultimately, this is just a fact of all-star life.

Train. Somewhere: As we've already covered, it is not – I repeat, *not* – important that your son is training at a brand-name, big-reputation training facility, but it's absolutely crucial that your son is getting ready for his pro day. If he's frustrated because his draft status isn't where he thought it would be, or because he didn't get an all-star invite, or because his teammates signed with splashy agents and he hasn't gotten the same treatment, he's got to move on. In some cases, schools will be having their pro days in the first week of March, and some even late February. Everything can change if your son goes out and really kills it at his workout. There's only one thing he'll be evaluated on between January and draft day, and that's his workout, whether it be at the combine or on campus. He needs to take it very seriously.

Hire representation: By mid-February, it's time to stop hoping that some big, fancy agent will come along offering high-end training and endless NFL connections. I've seen players who were on the bubble put off signing with an agent because they kept waiting for the absolutely perfect fit. That was a bad move. I guess, at the end of the day, if a player is really supreme, he doesn't need someone out there promoting him. Louisville QB **Lamar Jackson** went that route in the '18 draft, and he wound up going in the first round anyway. However, players who could use an extra push are best off having an advocate working for them. Remember, your son doesn't have to show cause to fire his agent. If he feels things aren't working; he can dump his representation at any time and only has to wait five days until he hires someone else. For that reason, he doesn't need to feel like he's signing his life away if things don't work. At the very least, he needs someone trying to get him into the best platform possible, usually involving his pro day.

Chapter 8
The Combine

Let's talk about one of the fundamental events of the draft cycle, the combine.

Which players, and how many, are invited to the combine? Around 350 players will go to Indianapolis in late February, but they won't all find out they got the call that month.

Combine invitations *used* to come in two waves, with the first wave for about 250 seniors in late December and the second wave of around 100 coming right after the early entries are certified in mid-January. Probably 25 or so members of the second wave were underclassmen who entered the draft early, and the rest were seniors who didn't make the cut the first time. However, those days are gone.

Big changes: Today, more and more underclassmen don't wait four years to come out. Instead, especially if they are running backs, they leave after three years, whether they are true juniors or redshirt sophomores. For the top offensive linemen, it's usually after their redshirt junior seasons. Perhaps as a result, the way players are invited has changed. Modern players start getting the good news in December. Actually, I should say their coaches find out. National Football Scouting (which chooses the invitees) began telling the coaches instead of the players directly in the last few years so they could hold the info until after bowl play. Since bowl play stretches from mid-December until early January, word leaks out for about a month on who's headed to Indy. Then, once the deadline for early entry passes, the league starts extensive background checks to make sure players have no domestic violence convictions or other major offenses. Invitations come out on a rolling basis through January and even early February, and the final list is finally published early that month.

How are players invited? National Football Scouting essentially holds a vote with representatives from each team so that there are 32 up or down votes. While the exact process still involves a good bit of mystery, NFS continues holding a majority vote on players until it gets to around 350. There's also a short list that NFS maintains of players who barely missed the cut, and those players are added when a player goes back to school or declines the invitation (which surprisingly happens, though rarely).

Can a good agent, or a well-connected coach, get a player invited? No. No matter how powerful your agent or how established your coach, you're pretty much out of luck if you want to lobby National to include a player. Jeff Foster, who heads National, is a no-nonsense kind of guy who doesn't play a lot of politics, much to his credit. That wasn't always true – believe it or not, 49ers head coach **Kyle Shanahan** made the 2003 combine list despite a whopping 33 receptions in four years at Duke and Texas as an undersized tight end. Foster's predecessor was a lot more open to being swayed by the old boy network. But no longer. So if your son's teammate tells you his agent told him he could get him into the combine, show him this book.

Who gets to go in and watch the proceedings? There are a limited number of tickets to get into Lucas Oil

Stadium, and though selected media get to go in and watch, most agents, trainers, financial professionals and marketing specialists crowd around televisions to watch their clients perform. Some college coaches and even some combine trainers can get guest passes, but it's not easy to get in. There was a time when it was easy to sneak into the stadium, but no more. But perhaps that's good. It's kind of fun and exciting for a while to watch grown men run 40 yards, but it wears thin pretty fast.

Quarterbacks as "throwers:" Once the full combine invitation list comes out, it will include around 20 passers. Three of them will be invited as "throwers." This means that though they are official invitees, they are only invited because they'll be throwing passes that running backs, receivers, tight ends and defensive backs run under during the full week of drills. They get to take their turns to run the 40, perform drills, and otherwise be tested alongside the other quarterbacks. But they have "extra" duties – although nowhere on the list do they have asterisks besides their names that indicates that. If your son isn't given a standard slot, but is asked to come as a thrower, jump on it. **Tony Romo** is one example of a player only invited to the combine as a thrower.

How many players by position are usually brought in to Indianapolis? There are no hard and fast rules, but here is the position-by-position breakdown over two recent combines (2011 and 2012):

Pos	'12	'11	Pos	'12	'11	Pos	'12	'11	Pos	'12	'11
CB	36	35	DT	30	27	OG	20	13	WR	49	46
FS	10	9	ILB	8	15	OT	28	33	TE	14	16
SS	12	10	OLB	23	19	RB	28	39	PK	5	5
DE	30	30	OC	6	9	QB	19	18	PT	6	4

There was also one long-snapper each of 2011 and 2012, and that trend has continued. It should also be noted that the total number of players has risen slightly over the years, though there are usually 325-350 players invited.

Is every player who goes to the combine drafted? No. Depending on the number of picks awarded due to teams based on free agent losses, there are usually around 255 players selected, which means that at a minimum, 80-100 combine picks don't get called on draft day. Usually, it's a little higher, between 100-125, who are snubbed.

Should I go to the combine if my son is invited? If your son gets the call and you insist on going, you might be disappointed. The combine is a mostly "closed" event, and there aren't a lot of opportunities to get past security if you don't have league credentials. If you go, be prepared to log a lot of hours at the Omni hanging around the Nike suite (it's free; you can even get a haircut, on the house, if you time it right), but don't expect to get into Lucas Oil Stadium. For the most part, only team personnel and a limited number of media members have that privilege. You're probably better off staying home.

Chapter 9
Evaluation

By February, despite what you might read on the Internet, there is only one more chance for NFL scouts to evaluate your son, and that's at his pro day (or at the combine). We'll take it from the top.

Last shot: Don't underestimate the importance of pro days and combine workouts. Yes, running, jumping, lifting, etc., is not the same thing as playing football, but your son can spark interest with scouts if he really tests well. I remember my first combine in 2003. Scouts were pouring out of the RCA Dome after wide receivers had run, and I remember a scout remarking that he had to take another look at the film of Texas A&M's **Bethel Johnson**. That new interest was the result of Johnson running a 4.38 40, and it's probably why he went on to be drafted in the second round by the Patriots despite a so-so college career.

Don't wait: Every year, during our all-star travels, we survey agents about their clients' pro days. During those January and sometimes early-February discussions, some agents still have no idea whether or not their schools will have NFL workouts. Make sure your son's agent knows all about his pro day as well as those nearby. Pro days are not mandatory, and some schools just don't see them as a priority. Others may schedule them, but keep it almost a secret.

Get the word out: The NFL has a daily email that goes out to all teams and it runs down all the latest pro day information. The league even maintains a secure website that houses all pro day info in one place. Despite this, scouts don't automatically know about schools' pro days. If your son's pro liaison coach hasn't informed the league of the school's pro day, there's a great chance no scouts will show up. Make sure, gently, that this doesn't happen with the coach who runs your son's pro day.

The date matters: Most likely, you have no control over when your son's school schedules his pro day, but if you do, push for no later than mid-March. The later the date, the better the chance your son's results get lost in the wash, and it's possible the workout might even get snubbed by scouts. If your son is from a smaller school and his pro day is set for April, do whatever you can to get it moved up. I texted several scouts one winter, asking them if later pro days could harm a prospect. One said flatly, "yes." The other said it might not harm a big-time player or one from a major school, but later dates – especially in April – definitely have an impact on lesser players at lesser schools. Teams have final scouting meetings in April, and sometimes pro days just slip through the cracks. A third disagreed, saying teams "go to schools for specific reasons, as much for off-field information as drills and tests." Still, I think smaller schools will always get overlooked and later dates make it more likely.

No guarantees: This is important to remember: Scouts are not mandated to attend pro days. As such, your son's school may host a workout that no teams send representatives to. This is especially dicey when your son's agent schedules a workout for your son, or when a school only holds a workout because you or an agent have been bugging a coach incessantly. Ultimately, your son's exposure may depend on how effectively his agent can communicate that he's working out. Usually, it's far better to get him to a workout that scouts will definitely attend.

Hard to move up: If your son attended an FBS school, relax. You can be assured that his pro day will have at least a few teams there. However, if your son attended a small school, the NFL allows him to work out at an FBS school in the state where he played. However, that school is not *required* to let him work out, and over the past decade, schools have become increasingly stingy about letting "outsiders" into their pro days. Coaches increasingly see small-school invitees as people who could potentially steal jobs from their own players. Or they see small-schoolers as hopeless dreamers. That's why most schools that allow players from outside colleges to work out ask for an NFL scout to call on the player's behalf. Some schools ask for *two* scouts to call, and some don't allow entry, no matter what.

So what do you do if your son is stuck at a school that may not get scouts' attention? Read on …

Recruiting scouts: If he's not highly rated, your son's last, best hope might involve his agent reaching out to scouts and semi-begging them to come to his workout. Keep in mind that agents in this predicament don't have a lot of leverage, so if your son gets as many as one scout, that's very good news. If there's one thing that scouts always complain about, it's the unlimited pleading emails they receive in March from agents hoping they'll attend a pro day.

Small-school notes: There are a couple of things to remember if your son isn't from an FBS school. There are several small schools in West Texas that annually get together (usually at Abilene Christian University) to hold a pro day. Similarly, schools from the Great Lakes Intercollegiate Athletic Conference (GLIAC) will also band together, and several small Arkansas schools do the same thing. This has become common practice for smaller conferences. Usually, it means they get at least some scout coverage because so many players are involved.

One final note: Just because your son attends a school with an elite prospect, that doesn't mean you'll be able to piggyback off of that interest. Often, a player will complete his workout at the combine, or have a personal pro day, which means the other players at the school can't draw flies (much less scouts) to the workout. So, know in advance if a high-visibility player is going to skip your son's workout.

Scouts can be funny: Not "ha ha" funny, but they do have their own little peculiarities. Here's an example. The 40-yard dash has become the accepted measure of baseline athleticism. Despite the seeming objectivity of this number, there is lots of subjectivity to its measurement. For example, you will never see schools time their players electronically at their pro days, no matter how much they've invested in technology. One reason for this is because electronic times are slower, but the other is because scouts *only* trust their own stopwatches. Everyone always wants to be able to time a kid for himself. Now, here's the dirty little secret: At the end of the day, when scouts gather to come up with an "official" time for a kid, they all chime in with the 40 time they each recorded.

Then whoever is running the workout takes the one in the middle, and that's the one they all write down in their notebooks as the player's "official" 40 time. I've seen this. Now try explaining that one.

Scouts may skew info for a player they like: Usually, this works in good ways, and scouts cover up bad numbers for players if they've grown attached to a young man and like his potential. I interviewed former Redskins scout Miller McCalmon at Rice University in the Ffll of 2014, and Miller discussed how he did exactly this for an Auburn running back, **Stephen Davis**, who went on to a 10-year career with the Redskins despite a lousy 40 time at his pro day. If Miller hadn't "fudged" Davis' 40 time, who knows if the 'Skins would have rolled the dice on him? There are similar stories in the book, *Al Davis: Behind the Raiders Shield.* Of course, I'd be crazy not to entertain the possibility that a scout's bias might also work *against* players the scout doesn't like, though I've never personally seen this.

A note about conditions and surfaces: You may be concerned because your son is going to be running in outdoor conditions and is subject to the elements. Unfortunately, if his team doesn't have an indoor facility or isn't willing to relocate to one nearby, there's little that can be done about this. It's encouraging that more and more pro days are being conducted indoors, which is something I've noticed as I've surveyed our notes and headlines from previous pro days. However, if that's not the case, scouts are pretty good about giving players a chance to run their first 40 against the wind and second with the wind. There is also a very detailed system for identifying the surface a player is running on. For example, if the surface is rubber, teams will add half a tenth of a second to a 40 time, whereas if it's grass, they'll cut time off a 40 to reflect a slower surface. It's imperfect, but it's better than nothing.

TEAM PRO DAYS

While schools' pro days have become pretty well-known to fans of the NFL draft and are even starting to be televised, NFL teams' local pro days have still been a little slow to gain traction. However, they're an accepted part of the evaluation process and it's important to know what they are.

The rules: The league allows all NFL teams to invite players who competed in high school or college within the metro area of the team, usually defined as 40 miles from city center (but technically defined as within the metro area by a Rand McNally road atlas – not kidding). However, there's a pretty generous "fudge factor" at play here, because the NFL doesn't strictly regulate a city's borders. I've seen teams go far outside the normal "metro" boundaries to invite "local" players.

What happens?: Generally, these workouts are half-goodwill gesture/half serious workout and evaluation tool. Most teams print up T-shirts for the participants and some provide full workout apparel with logo. Some include interviews and other off-field elements, and some even request that players take drug tests. However, the one thing all teams do is measure and weigh, then go through a usual pro day with 40s, jumps, drills, the works. Usually, a team's entire scouting staff watches or at least passes through during the workout. It's basically like taking a proctored test. A team gets to take one last look at local players, either to verify what they've seen or to completely rule them out. By the way, there are success stories. Longtime NFL WR **Miles Austin** signed with the Cowboys as an undrafted free agent on the strength of his performance at the team's workout, and the 'Boys also brought in former Patriots WR **Wes Welker**, though they passed on him in the draft and in post-draft free agency.

Who holds them?: Even though this is an easy chance to sift for hidden gems, not all teams hold them. The Seahawks, Bills, Broncos, Jaguars and Steelers are teams that haven't traditionally held such workouts, and the Packers, Redskins and Vikings are other teams that don't consider team pro days as a fixture of the evaluation process. Generally, a team that's not in a major metro market doesn't host a workout.

How do invitations work?: For the most part, teams do their own research and invite players based on their interests. However, there are plenty of instances where agents were able to get their clients into a workout. The key is knowing when they're being held, how to contact teams, and having the persistence to keep trying until there's an answer or an invite. If your son is eligible to attend such a workout, make sure his agent is working to make this happen.

Chapter 10
March and April

So many things happen in the last 60 days before the draft that we wanted to dedicate a chapter to it.

"UGLY" PARENTS

I usually attend 2-3 pro days each March just to stay in touch with my clients, get out of the office and maybe learn something. At times, I get to see something I've never seen before, as I did in March 2015.

Advocates: Before I go on, I want to tell you that I admire any parent who strongly encourages his son's dreams. Any young man who gets reasonably close to playing in the NFL deserves the full support of his parents. At times, that may involve more than just emotional support. Ultimately, I think most parents feel it's worth it to exhaust every possibility just to make sure no stone is left unturned. Still, there's a line you shouldn't cross, and I saw two well-meaning parents come really close to it.

Showtime: These days, it's certainly not unusual to see parents filming their sons' workouts with their camera phones, but these parents took it to another level. The father had a camera set up on a tripod that he continually moved from one side of the field to another, capturing multiple angles of the young man's workout. After conversations with people familiar with the parents, it became pretty clear this behavior wasn't out of character.

Steering clear: I noticed that this player was wearing a T-shirt associated with one of my trainer clients, so I texted the trainer, seeking more info. He replied with this caution: "His mom is a little out there. If u start a conversation be prepared for at least 30 min lol.' No problem. I had already ducked her. When many parents find out what I do, they want to buttonhole me about their son, hoping I can do something to enhance his NFL chances. But in this case, I became alarmed/amused when I saw the head coach and an assistant take an out-of-their-way route back to the team's offices. "They're going that way so they don't bump into the parents," one of the coaches told me. It was at this point it made sense that the player's agent was a no-show at the pro day, a true rarity. Undoubtedly, he knew what he was doing.

Contract matters: Unfortunately, that meant the parents had to impose on a good-natured contract advisor at the workout to discuss their questions related to the player's SRA (standard representation agreement). This agent was supposed to join us for lunch; about 15 minutes after what was supposed to have been a five-minute conversation, I departed, along with the other members of the lunch party. I have no idea how long he talked to them about a pretty cut-and-dried, simple document.

The lesson: I don't mean to ridicule parents who are taking their son's NFL chances seriously. However, I would caution them, or anyone, to understand that people in college and pro football have a limited bandwidth. For them to properly do their jobs, they need to be given a little space. I hope parents realize that.

DON'T DO THESE THINGS

By March, you're about eight weeks from the draft. There's a good chance parents and players are confused, frustrated, and maybe even lost by the process. Despite your confusion, keep a few dos and don'ts in mind. First, the don'ts.

Don't worry about the combine: Your son may still be nursing frustration that an invitation to Indy never came. Don't worry about it. Pro days start in March, and a player who goes out and tears it up at pro day doesn't need to worry about a combine snub. A great 40, a great 3-cone, a great broad jump are the same no matter if it took place in Indianapolis or on campus, as long as there are scouts there to chronicle it.

Don't compare your numbers to the numbers of other players: By March, everyone knows what players had great results in Indy and which ones didn't. Pretty soon, you'll have your own results to compare to them. Be careful about being too "literal" about your son's numbers. The good news is that some teams keep a place on their draft board for outstanding pro day performances and give priority during the post-draft period to signing such players. However, I've never heard of a player moving ahead of a combine invitee based solely on his runs, jumps and drills. There's not a direct relationship between a player's pro day results and his NFL prospects. It's just not that simple.

Don't Google your son's name: OK, maybe it's too much to ask not to do this at all, but do the best you can not to pin all your son's draft hopes on moving up the board on NFL Draft Scout or Rotoworld or your favorite draft site. The media only get a very limited view of what is on teams' draft boards. While some scouting directors and GMs provide inside information to the better-connected draft analysts out there, most draft gurus are making best guesses and rating players based on their own evaluation. Legitimate NFL draft prospects and their agents start to get plenty of calls in March and April.

DO THESE THINGS

Granted, your son has an NFLPA-licensed contract advisor who is handling the business of football for him. Still, you don't want to leave things to chance. Here are a few things to keep in mind as March arrives.

Know who else is working out at your son's pro day (passers/position mix): It's important to have a good passer at your pro day. This is especially important if your son is a receiver, tight end, running back, defensive back or anyone who needs to catch or run under passes during the workout. If you have a subpar quarterback there, or worse, no quarterback at all (meaning a scout will have to throw passes), it could lead to a lousy workout, though it's not your son's fault. Make sure these questions are asked well before pro day starts. There are pretty strict rules about who can participate at these workouts, so you'll want to make sure everything is ironed out in advance.

Know who else is working out at your son's pro day (draft status): The number of "sexy" players at your son's pro day is just as important as making sure you have the right mix of players by position. I'm always talking to agents who are excited that their client's school has a combine invitee, ensuring that there will be several scouts around to watch and record pro day. That's not necessarily true. Though usually a combine invitee will return to campus to conduct positional drills for scouts, many times such athletes will complete their workouts in Indianapolis, leaving nothing to draw scouts to their school's pro day. NFL teams know this, and this could lead some of them to skip your son's pro day. That's not good news for the players hoping to ride a star's coattails.

Know what scouts will be at your pro day: One of the things we feature at Inside the League is a grid that breaks down all 32 teams' scouts by region, placing them all in their assigned areas. It's not a bad thing to know which scout, exactly, will be at your son's pro day, and it's not hard to predict if you know who's assigned where. Agents who do their homework in advance might find an angle, a reason for a scout to like a player. Maybe it's a common alma mater, or a common high school, or hometown, or fraternity, or almost anything. Remember, the human element often comes into play during the evaluation process. It's also good to know what teams have needs at your son's position. Your son needs an agent who won't be caught unprepared when it comes to research.

COMPARISONS

In March and April, you're going to hear and read things about players your son played against or perhaps played with. You might also see players with very similar stats and/or height, weight and speed that mirror your son's numbers, and wonder why that player is getting big publicity and acclaim, while your son is not. Maybe you and your son have been struggling with this for a while now. It can be very frustrating.

Numbers: There are several reason two similar players can look very different in the eyes of NFL teams. Let's start by comparing production. One player might be a physical specimen, perfect in every way with incredible workout numbers – but not be able to put it together on the field. These players are often the stars of March after having been skipped over the previous December and January when all-star slots were being handed out. On the other hand, some players are pedestrian in their workouts but were stellar producers on the field. These players tend to gain momentum in January, but often get mired in a "slump" in March. That's because, in general, all-star spots are handed out based on college production, but pro days are all about projection and what could happen if a skilled coaching staff turns a player's potential into production.

Conferences and geographical areas: During the run-up to the 2015 draft, I tried hard to get a young man into an all-star game I was assisting with. I lobbied hard for him to get an invitation, and he should have, but ultimately did not. I'm pretty sure I know why. Very simply, he played at a non-sexy school in an area of the country not known for producing top prospects. If, in the 21st century, you don't think your son can be overlooked, you're wrong. If you play in some parts of the Southwest (New Mexico, West Texas, or areas of Arizona and Nevada) or the upper Northwest (Idaho, the Dakotas, Utah, Montana), you will have far fewer eyes on you. Chances are good that the scouts who evaluated your son won't "jump on the table" to advocate for your son in the war room because, traditionally, difference-makers come from the Southeast. The same is true if you came from a lesser FBS conference or a small school. You're not going to get the same attention from the media, either, so don't get too worked up about it.

Preferences: Ten years ago, safeties were seen as failed cornerbacks. They were not given priority on draft day. Then slot receivers became popular, and everyone needed a guy who could play up in the box and tackle well but also cover the slot. Safeties became a priority. Similarly, tweener-type tight ends were seen as having no value. Then the idea of a "move" tight end became popular, and now those are priority players, too. Your son may be on the wrong side of a trend. On the other hand, maybe a new trend will develop in this draft (they tend to develop every few years). Bottom line, your son is subject to the changing whims of NFL teams.

One more thing: I heard a coach once compare scouts to teenagers at a high school dance. They ask the hottest girls to dance first, then settle for the less-sexy-but-more-reliable girls later. The draft is a lot like this. A scout is willing to take a chance on a player that checks all the boxes even when he's not a great player. It's entirely defensible, and if it works out, he could look like a genius. It's not until a few rounds later that he picks the guys who can really be the backbone of the team. It's just part of that human element that makes the draft mysterious and unpredictable. Some find it charming, others vexing.

SHOULD I GO TO THE DRAFT?

You may be thinking about heading to the NFL draft, especially if you live near where the draft will be held, or if you think your son might be go in the early rounds. I don't think it's smart.

By invitation only: When the draft was in New York every year, especially in the 1980s and 1990s, it was relatively easy to get tickets to the draft. After all, it was a big benefit to ESPN's cameras to have colorfully dressed Jets and Giants fans booing or celebrating the picks. Today, with the draft going on the road, it's still relatively easy to attend the draft, but with the exception of a few NFL-related things to do downtown, access to the real work of the draft will be limited. You're not going to get any insights into your son's draft prospects or enhance his draft status by going to the draft.

An event for the fans: As we alluded to above, most everything that goes on around the draft is fan-related. You're not a fan. You are, potentially, connected to a future NFL player. It makes a lot more sense to stay close to home in my estimation. This is especially true if a team needs to contact your son on draft day regarding his selection or perhaps being signed as an undrafted free agent. You'll want to be somewhere free of distractions. Speaking of distractions …

An unnecessary distraction: At the 2015 NFL Combine, my wife and I were at Velocity, an upscale bar at the J.W. Marriott Hotel in Indianapolis and a popular hangout for NFL types during the combine. While there, I saw one top prospect for the draft whose parents and their friends formed a party of 10-12 people, just hanging out and holding court. I remember seeing them standing around in full regalia with the young man's agent nearby, looking a little nervous and distracted by it all. They seemed like nice people (I met some of them), but the point is, that player's agent had a lot better uses for his time than fielding texts from the entourage members and making sure they got reservations at St. Elmo's. I could tell numerous stories about players' parents who did similar things at the Senior Bowl, the draft, or other places along the evaluation timeline. Teams really do talk to agents about players during this time. It's not smart to get in the way of that.

But I missed all the other stuff!: If your son makes it to the league, there will be countless opportunities to enjoy the lifestyle of an NFL player. There will be games, parties, the Super Bowl, and many other exclusive events. None of them will interfere with your son's chances of playing in the league. Until then, I recommend you stay close to home and leave the celebration for after the draft.

PERSPECTIVE

By March, you're getting a real look at how teams have evaluated your son. Hopefully there has been legitimate interest. Maybe it's been a little slow, but I hope you've been able to maintain your poise regardless of how things have turned out. Here are two examples: One is of a father who will likely have a really tough draft weekend, and the other dad is one who is going to be fine.

Father 1: One father called one fall to interview me before consenting to receive our free newsletter. His son was most likely a camp guy, though I didn't dare tell him that. From the moment we started talking, I knew he was skeptical that I had anything to offer. He'd ask a question and I'd answer it, followed by a long pause, as if he weren't impressed. At one point he asked how I got paid, even though I had already told him (over and over) that what we were discussing came with no obligations whatsoever. When I finally conceded that my service was subscriber-financed – though that was completely separate from the free newsletter – he chuckled. I guess he was looking for an apology for my running a for-profit service. But that's not what bothered me. What bothered me was that when we were finishing things up – with me patiently reiterating that while there is plenty of draft information on the web, the data I was offering was tailor-made for him – he was pretty dismissive. "There's lots of information on the Internet, and you can find anything," he assured me. "The problem is finding out what's reliable and what isn't." We closed with him informing me that he'd talk to his son and that they would decide if the promise of my (did I say free?) newsletter was worth their time. It didn't surprise me that I never got that phone call. By the way, his son went undrafted and unsigned. I still think I could have helped them.

Father 2: I spoke to the second father around October, and before we did, I called around and did a little legwork on where his son stood as a prospect. As I feared, I got back that his son is a solid college player who probably figured as a late-rounder or perhaps a priority free agent. When we got to the part where I wanted to offer up the scouts' opinion, I remember wincing as I began. How would he react? What would his response be? I was pleasantly surprised. "That's pretty much what we expected," he said. The rest of our conversation continued in that vein, with him asking detailed questions about the process and my opinion on a smart course of action. It was refreshing to speak to a parent who is invested in his son's career, but clearly hasn't put blinders on. He knows and values the opportunity that's ahead for his son and realizes not to take it for granted. Maybe that's what makes me the most frustrated by the other father.

Bottom line: As a father myself, I try to remember that the things that make my boys special to my wife and me are maybe not so unique among all teenage boys. Similarly, the number of young men who've had a little college success and aspire to an NFL career is pretty commonplace. is *not* rare. Do the best you can to be reasonable in your approach and understand that the place your son wants to be isn't assured. It will make things a lot easier if he hits bumps in the road.

FINANCES

As you wait for your son's pro day, or wait for the draft if his pro day is over, you may find yourself asking, is there anything I can do to help? That's why March and April might be a good time to start thinking about financial planners.

Isn't it a bit early?: Yes, probably. Your son isn't even on an NFL roster yet. Why does he need to be thinking about wealth managers? My feeling is that this isn't a good time to be making a such a decision, but it's not a bad time to start doing a little vetting. Maybe you already have a financial expert who handles your personal finances, but even if you do, why not start talking to a few more people? At worst, you're starting your homework long before the test," and at best, you're helping your son vet key people while simultaneously helping you burn off some of the nervous energy you're experiencing during this time.

A key role: I always describe one of the primary differences between agents and financial planners is that players often want to be the sole decision-maker on their agent choice, but they look for all the counsel they can get from their parents when it comes to selecting a financial advisor. It's also pretty common to ask around with former teammates.

Does experience matter?: I've gotten really mixed answers from parents and agents on this. On one hand, NFL players are paid in different ways than your traditional 40-hours-per-week worker. They're taxed in different ways, too. They look at buying and selling property vs. renting differently. In short, there are many different philosophies and situations they'll face. But at the end of the day, it's all about being smart and responsible with money. One way or another, all good financial advisors can help a well-intentioned young man make good decisions.

All about trust: Virtually everyone who approaches you about working with your son knows money. Some may have more money under management, and some may be independent while others are with major investing houses. Ultimately, you're going to want your son to have chemistry with the best candidate, and make sure he's credible. Of course, you should still run every candidate through FINRA BrokerCheck. You can never be too careful, and even though the NFLPA vets and registers financial planners. Many of the ones involved in financial controversies with NFL players (Google **Jeff Rubin** and **Hodge Brahmbhatt**) held a players association certification. Also, remember that a financial planner whose name doesn't show up in FINRA shouldn't be presumed clean. It may be that he's not registered with the appropriate licensing bodies, so they don't even recognize him as a financial professional.

WHAT ARE YOU HEARING?

From time to time on social media, I'll see an article that lists the percentages of high school athletes who go on to compete in college, followed by the percentage of college athletes playing professionally. According to a study conducted by the NCAA, college football players have a 1.6 percent chance of getting drafted into the NFL. It got me thinking about the narrowing-down process that takes place during the pre-draft phase. When March is over, the last real evaluation has taken place for the vast majority of draft-eligible players. Let's discuss some topics related to the time between pro day and draft day.

Standards: For most of the year, scouts cover the nation with a fine-toothed comb trying to measure the three pillars of competency for all potential draftees, which are size, athleticism (i.e., 40 time) and college production. By mid-April, most teams will also agree on the 500 or so pro prospects who will be in NFL camps after the draft. With the end of pro days, things will really be pretty cut and dried. No amount of emails, phone calls or social media work by an agent can get a player into that group of 500-600 players. Your son may be tempted to call or text his agent daily, maybe hourly, asking "what are you hearing?" This is unlikely to bear fruit. More than likely, if your agent sees any signs of NFL interest, you and your son are not going to have to wait for a call.

Due diligence: For the most part, if a player is in that group of 500-600 players, he's going to be hearing from teams in late March and throughout April. Teams will want to verify his contact info, make sure they know where he'll be on draft day, and who his agent is. They'll also want to bring him in for extra workouts or meetings, getting to know him better. They may also express interest, hoping to persuade him to snub offers from other teams during the post-draft frenzy. Many teams get aggressive, putting together emails or YouTube presentations touting the number of undrafted free agents who routinely make their respective teams. Bottom line, if your son is under consideration for an NFL camp, it will not come as a surprise on draft day.

No calls: If all of these communications are not happening over the two weeks before the draft, it probably means draft day is going to be a quiet one. I certainly hope I'm wrong if this applies to your son, but in most cases, I won't be. I'm not telling you this to douse your son's hopes, but I do want to be as real, genuine and authentic as I possibly can be. There is a time for accepting the reality of the situation, and I don't want that time to come abruptly when the last pick comes off the board. I just want you to be prepared for every circumstance.

I'm not here: Scouts tend to get a little shifty in the late spring. Here's an illustration. In the spring of 2015, Norfolk State had a pro day that was widely attended by NFL personnel due to the presence of DE **Lynden Trail**. Not surprisingly, the local paper covered it. At some point, a photographer took a picture and wanted to identify the scout in the shot, but the scout wouldn't identify himself. The photographer wasn't seeking any inside information, just a name. Sound a little paranoid? It probably is, but this isn't that unusual. One spring, I got an email from an agent in the West who'd met a scout at a pro day but didn't ever get his last name (first name only). My client was hoping I could figure out who it was. This happens all the time.

Locked doors: I always encourage agents (young ones, especially) to "work the crowd" as much as possible on a pro day – hand out cards to scouts and introduce themselves. After all, at a pro day, an agent not only has face time but also has currency with teams. That's why scouts are there, right? But there are hang-ups with that strategy. Some scouts are friendly and engaging, but others are outright hostile. You're also going to get overly eager sports information types who shoo anyone away from scouts if they get too close. The other issue is that many teams take an "all hands on deck" approach to scouting, sending out everyone from the director of college scouting to the janitor (almost) to get times and measurements. These folks offer varying levels of access, influence and proficiency. It's always good for agents to make a contact with a team, but not all contacts are created equal.

Seasonal: There's also the issue of time of year. In the fall, scouts are pretty willing to talk, at least to agents they know and with whom they have a comfort level. The reason is that their job is to find every player who might have NFL ability. With only 24 hours in a day, scouts don't attend every school and watch every workout. They need "bird dogs" out there helping them turn up prospects, and in some cases, agents fit the bill. However, as fall turns to winter and winter to spring, scouts tend to play their cards a little closer to the vest. It's generally accepted that, after pro days and about 2,500 players work out, there's less fear that there are undiscovered gems out there. Also, at this time, scouts are no longer driving around, staying at hotels, and watching film at schools. They don't have long stretches to talk or have the independence that comes while being on the road. In April, scouts are mostly sitting in meetings all day, surrounded by their bosses and other scouts.

ON MARKETING

Sometimes parents ask me how their sons can make money off the field. How much, if any, can be expected? Is there a bundle of cash out there to be made?

Lonely at the top: If your son is going to be a top-10 draft pick, his agent is going to be sorting through plenty of off-the-field offers during the run-up to the draft. For those players who are selected by teams in major markets (especially New York, Chicago and maybe Washington), there will be an uptick of offers after the draft, especially when it comes to early picks. For everyone else, there's not a whole lot. This is why, chances are, you don't need a separate marketing agent to get you through the draft.

Hidden talents: There are a couple of reasons why NFL players get passed up for the big marketing dollars. One reason is that in golf, boxing, tennis and other individual sports, there's only one person making things happen. In football, there are 22 men on the field at any one time. The other reason is that football players essentially hide their faces from the viewing public. That makes it very hard to get to know players the way baseball and basketball fans do. You may be old enough to remember when Cowboys running back **Emmitt Smith** used to remove his helmet as soon as he scored a touchdown. The reason wasn't strictly ego and fame; it was also to establish a marketing presence.

What's left?: If your son is slated to go in the top 200 picks in the draft, regardless of his position, he's got trading card money coming his way. This could number in the hundreds of thousands of dollars (if he's a first-rounder and/or if he plays quarterback, running back or wide receiver), or could be in the tens of thousands (if he's going in the third or fourth round, or if he plays defense). From there, it's a little dicey. Sometimes, if he has an aggressive agent, he can get a public signing show in his hometown or the town where he went to college, but that's not a given. He also might get free clothing and shoes from one of the major athletic apparel companies, but there's not much money being offered by these firms, which is quite the reversal from the early-to-mid-2000s when there was plenty of money being thrown around. If your son is just hoping to get drafted, set the marketing thoughts aside. I was able to see the money that was *turned down* by a Patriots player in February 2015, fresh off a Patriots Super Bowl win; he had once been a marginal prospect in the 2009 draft who no one could have conceived of being a spokesman for a company or signing autographs for money. A big win in Glendale, Ariz., changed all that. Believe me, the cash he passed up was substantial. Tell your son to focus on making a roster. After that, good things could be on the way.

STARTING OVER

As a young man moves from pro football to college, everything changes. That includes lifestyle. The details of changing addresses, moving household items, signing a lease, moving cars across-country, etc., are often viewed as taking care of themselves, but that's not always true. If your son missed details like this or turns them over to his agent without following up, he could wind up with unsatisfying results.

In an attempt to prepare you for everything your son may face, I asked Chris Dingman of The Dingman Group to address this topic. I've come to rely on Chris, who founded and owns the leading player relocation service in the business. His thoughts on the fundamentals of relocation, moving, renting and other such topics are what informs my thoughts on this topic.

Before I go any further, let me answer a question I get at times: Doesn't the NFL handle moves, relocation, and the like? What you need to know is that all teams have someone on staff (sometimes called the Director of Player Programs, or the Director of Player Engagement, or some other title) whose job is to help players with off-the-field issues such as relocation, legal entanglements and anything in between. Some of the people in these positions are quite good and take their jobs very seriously. Others are ex-athletes given a job due to their history with the team or standing in the community. Very often, there's high turnover at this position, leading to instability and a shortfall in professionalism and competence. Your son might wind up with a team that has a good person in this position, but it's better to know the drill in case he doesn't.

The basics: Whether entering the NFL as a drafted player or an undrafted free agent, relocation is imminent. Once your son makes an NFL roster, the relocation process is more or less identical for both. The only difference may be the time of year you relocate or begin the relocation process. Whether you get drafted to the San Francisco 49ers or Indianapolis Colts, the typical needs of a new NFL player during relocation are as follows:

1. Buy or rent a home
2. Ship household goods
3. Transport a vehicle(s)

Remember: When planning your relocation be mindful of your contract status and key NFL dates (OTAs, training camp and preseason). Realize that anything can happen. While it's very difficult to see the future, there are steps you can take to limit expenses or losses when making relocation decisions.

One size doesn't fit all: Each player's circumstances are different. Some have a family and some don't. The key is to determine the smartest time to make a commitment on a home to rent or purchase based on your contract status, depth chart and team situation. Usually, a young drafted player has personal items in his college residence. Sometimes, he has the foresight to place such items in storage until his pro team is known. Once a player knows the city he'll be playing in, it's time to decide on buying or renting. Players drafted early with significant guaranteed money have buying as an option. Otherwise it's highly recommended that a player rent for 9-12 months.

Long and short of it: Always consider offseason plans when locking in a year-long lease. If time is spent in your hometown or a city/state outside where you play, the home rented will be vacant while you still pay rent. Meanwhile, you'll also be renting or sharing space with someone in the city where you live/train in the offseason. There are always opportunities to manage expenses.

The order of things: Once a player gets drafted or signs after the draft, usually the first service that's initiated is the vehicle transport. After that, there's a home/apartment rental or purchase, and finally, the household goods get delivered. The vehicles may arrive prior to the selection of a residence while the player is looking for a residence with an assigned real estate agent. Once a residence is locked in, that's the perfect time to get the household goods packed and moved.

No free ride: According to the Collective Bargaining Agreement, drafted players and free agents are responsible for all costs associated with relocation. It's only when a team trades for a player that the team is obligated to pay relocation costs. It's important to budget for a relocation in advance.

THE END GAME

Everyone knows about the draft, but there's plenty to know about entering the league as an undrafted free agent or on a tryout basis. Here's a general overview.

The draft: This is the one everyone knows about. Every year, there are about 250 picks (the exact number varies based on free agent losses). Most players who are picked make the 53-man roster or at least the practice squad, though every year, several seventh-rounders, a handful of sixth-rounders and maybe 1-2 fifth-rounders get cut. Draftees almost always wind up on another team, at least on the practice squad.

Undrafted free agency: This is a misunderstood and even mysterious part of the process because teams approach the post-draft signing period in different ways. Bottom line, every draft-eligible player who isn't selected is part of the mad post-draft rush. It's like a shopping spree for players, all conducted by phone, and often with several "shoppers" representing each team. About 10 years ago, the post-draft bazaar was completed by midnight on the night of the draft, but the last 5-6 years, the bargaining has continued for up to 72 hours, and sometimes even longer. Still, the biggest names go quickest, and the longer the wait, the less chance a player has of landing a signing bonus. After about two hours, most of the big money is spent and the bigger names are signed. Anything north of $10,000 qualifies as a good bonus, and suggests that the signing team is going to give a player a real shot at making the roster. I haven't done a study of the odds of making a team for undrafted free agents, but I've always heard that the chances are about one in eight (about 12 percent) that a UDFA will make a team's

53. Most teams sign 10-12 undrafted free agents after the draft. Often, they sign players from their region, mainly to throw a local school a bone; obviously, some teams take this part of the draft more seriously than others. On the other hand, a smart contract advisor can really give his client a leg up on making a team if he manages the UDFA process wisely. Many agents would rather their clients go undrafted rather than to get selected in the seventh round; that way they can control where their players go.

Tryout, or three-day mini-camp invitees: Getting invited in for a tryout is better than nothing at all, but only by a little. Not all teams have tryout camps, but the ones that do will invite another 10-12 players to camp without a contract, and these players compete for a deal. Usually one, sometimes two, will earn a contract from these camps, but only rarely do they actually make a 53-man roster or a practice squad. Tryouts are conducted in shorts and helmets only (no pads). Usually, teams seek lights-out athletes who can make it on pure talent, then be molded into difference-makers. They run through drills over a long weekend, and the team's coaches and scouts try to identify players with undeniable athletic ability. Those players may be offered an undrafted free agent deal. There are such success stories – Titans CB **Malcolm Butler** originally entered the NFL as a tryout player with the Patriots, bucking those long odds. Getting invited in for a tryout is kind of like winning a lottery for the chance to win another lottery. You almost have to hit the jackpot twice to make a roster.

MONEY MATTERS

The hard truth in April is that if your son is not getting attention from NFL teams, odds are he will not be drafted or invited to a camp. That means he's in a category where he needs to improve/reinvent himself. Beware – there are lot of ways people try to make money off that desperation.

All-star games: I got a call from an agent one spring who asked if he should send a client to a certain all-star game the weekend of April 25-26. In other words, just a few days before the draft starts. The organizers of this game charge a fee for participation, and a player must cover his own transportation costs. If you haven't already figured it out, I *do not* recommend your son play in this game. First off, as a general rule, scouts are not going to attend an all-star game that's not in January (no matter what the all-star game's website says). No. 2, by the last weekend in April, teams' draft boards are already complete. Stay away.

Open tryouts (CFL): Most CFL teams hold pay-to-participate workouts in various markets (generally in the South) from February to May. Going to an open tryout is one way of getting a CFL camp invite, though the primary way CFL teams scout players is by watching players who attend NFL camps, then signing them after cuts. There are several negatives if your son goes to a tryout. For example, the odds are very, very long that he'll be signed, and most of the times I've attended such workouts, no one is signed. Another negative: these workouts do very little to evaluate a player as a football player. Coaches will be looking for raw athleticism and nothing more, so if your son is one of those guys who's better in pads than in shorts, he might get overlooked. Another negative: if your son *does* beat the odds and make a CFL team, he will be asked to sign a two-year deal. It's not optional. There is no way to go to the CFL, spend a season, then come back for an NFL tryout unless the CFL team releases the player. Regarding the finances, almost all CFL workouts are $100, cash only, though I've seen $80 workouts in some places, especially for those who register early. And, oh, by the way: before sending your son to a CFL tryout, understand that he's going to need a passport if he earns a contract. Most CFL teams are not going to offer a lot of assistance. With that I think when I got my passport near Houston in 2014 it cost about $150 and took 2-3 weeks for delivery. This is why, if you think the CFL is the best option for your son but don't want to buy a passport yet, make sure he hits a tryout in early April at the latest. That way he has time to get his papers before camp starts in May. Workouts such as these are a last resort. Good things happen occasionally to players who attend these workouts, but not often. We'll talk in more detail about the CFL a little later in this book.

Open tryouts (Arena): CFL teams aren't the only ones holding paid tryouts in the spring. The Arena Football League (AFL) teams, as well as other non-AFL indoor leagues that have sprung up across the nation, are doing the same. As I write this in the summer of 2018, it looks like the sun may be setting on indoor football. The AFL has dwindled to just a handful of teams, and the money being paid to players is minimal. With that said, your son may still find a tryout for one of these teams somewhere online or he might hear about one from a buddy. Costs will be about the same as they are for the CFL, but the payoff is a lot smaller. Most of these leagues are very unstable, and teams (and even leagues) go out of business at a moment's notice.

The indoor game is also different from the outdoor game in ways – style of play, roster size, field size, rules -- that go beyond the scope of this book. I have friends who work in indoor football who I have a lot of respect for, but my observation is that it's a dying sport. We'll go into more detail about arena football later.

Other open tryouts: Many services offer a combine / workout / tryout in the spring, promising that multiple CFL and AFL teams will attend. I don't recommend these workouts. They are just too plentiful and often don't deliver on their guarantees. Usually they're pretty vague about the representatives from teams attending. In any case, don't chase open tryouts endlessly. Set a budget of $200-$300 tops and stick to it. If it's not to be, no sense spending a king's ransom.

Chapter 11
Other Leagues And Non-NFL Football Ventures

Just because your son doesn't make it to the NFL doesn't mean he can't play football for a living. If he has a passion for the game and is willing to put off the rest of his life temporarily, there are opportunities as long as he understands these leagues are far less stable and decidedly less lucrative than playing on Sundays.

THE CFL

Before the arrival of the AAF, the XFL, and the Spring League, everybody's backup plan was the CFL. For many, it still is, so it bears discussing.

The basics of evaluation and rosters: By the middle of May, the CFL's draft is complete, and most teams have their rosters mostly formed. Any additions to their rosters come from agents sending film or video links to scouting contacts, as well as the odd player identified at a pay workout. Most CFL scouts are based in the United States, so players who scouts might want to take a last look at will mostly need to get in front of teams' evaluators at their own expense. On the other hand, CFL teams rely strongly on their U.S. agent contacts and give them the benefit of the doubt when they're trying to fill holes in their respective rosters.

Contracts: As we've already discussed, a player can't spend a season up north before hopping back down south to continue his NFL career. Standard deals are for two years, with the second season at the team's option. Most players in their first season will make about $45,000 for six months of work after taxes. Of course, some players may make more if they come in as a starter, but not a lot more. A good agent can usually negotiate a little more for a food allowance or lodging, but their client isn't looking at big bucks.

Training camp: Camps start a few weeks after the NFL draft and last only about two weeks, followed by another two weeks of preseason games, and then it's time for the season to kick off right around the middle of June. This is why, if your son thinks the CFL may be his best bet, he can't dawdle. He must be proactive about it in April, maybe even March.

Best positions: As we've noted in the pages of our newsletters, CFL teams look to fill their speed positions with U.S. players. That means defensive back, wide receiver, offensive tackle, defensive end, running back and maybe linebacker are going to be populated by players from the U.S. Interior offensive linemen and defensive linemen, plus fullback, safety, tight end / H-back and kickers and punters, are usually home-grown.

Neg lists: All CFL teams have "negotiation lists" for players that are not on their rosters. These players could be on NFL rosters (for instance, the story goes that **Tom Brady** is on a CFL neg list) or floating around as street free agents. These lists reserve a limited number of players for specific teams when they aren't under contract to other teams. It's mostly good news if you find out your son is on a team's neg list. The bad news is that these lists aren't published, so finding out your son's status is not easy. Usually, the best thing is simply to have his agent reach out to CFL teams and inquire about their interest; usually if your son is on a list, one of the teams will let you know – though chances are good they won't tell you exactly *which* team's list. Presuming your son does find out which team holds his negotiation rights, the team has a limited time to make him an offer, and once that time expires, he becomes free to negotiate with all CFL teams. I've heard lots of stories about teams handling this in a less-than-professional manner and trying to dodge their responsibilities here, so make sure your son's agent stays on the team that holds his rights. The good news is that neg lists are pretty limited, up to 45 players only. The bad news is that there's absolutely no accountability for teams because it's so shadowy. I've been working in the football business for almost two decades and I still don't have a clear understanding of how neg lists work.

One last thing: If your son's agent isn't CFL-certified, his agent isn't precluded from promoting your son up north. However, he *is* precluded from being listed as his contract advisor, so he can't charge fees.

The AAF

When the Alliance of American Football first announced its plans for launch in early 2018, I was pretty dismissive. Several months later, though there are still plenty of questions, I'm a lot more optimistic about the league's prospects.

The basics: Eight teams of 50 players each will play a 10-week season that wraps up over draft weekend in late April. Players will sign three-year deals that could earn them $250,000, and like the Arena League, pay will come through the AAF, not the actual teams. So if a franchise has sagging attendance or limited sponsorships, players will still get paid. Also, as in the Arena League, players can walk away if they get an NFL contract offer.

Worth taking seriously: The league will kick off after the 2019 Super Bowl, which means it's basically going from league announcement to league play in less than a year. I think that's a real positive in that many past leagues set a kickoff date far in the future because, I believe, it's fun to announce a league but much harder to actually spend the money and do the work. Virtually all steps the league's organizers have taken so far have shown that this is a league to be taken seriously.

A big squeeze: There are far fewer people who can play football competently than there are those who think they can. The rise of the AAF, a competent NFL alternative, is really going to impact other leagues and football ventures from a talent perspective. That's to say nothing of the eyeballs and dollars that will be drawn away from those other ventures.

The XFL

Though the rebirth of the XFL is even farther on the horizon than the AAF as this book goes to press, it looks like it will make it to the field and maybe even become viable for a period of time. So, let's take a look at it.

One and done: The XFL's first go-round was in 2001, and as everyone around the game knows, despite a fan-based approach and some interesting innovations, it lasted only one season. The media were truly merciless in their criticism of the league. I've always felt part of that was because the NFL was nervous over **Vince McMahon's** deep pockets and felt the league could perhaps be a threat. The league deserves more credit than it got, and you have to hand it to McMahon for landing a full season of broadcasts on a major network. Though the quality of play was obviously not NFL level, it was not as bad as its critics made it appear.

Take 2: The next round of XFL play is scheduled to kick off in 2020. We still don't know markets, salaries or roster sizes; all we know is that eight teams will play for 10 weeks. At any rate, based on the hires McMahon has made and the money he's already invested in the league, I think it's a go. That's good news for anyone who wants to play football professionally.

The timing is right: I should mention that the XFL will kick off just as the NFL could be facing a work stoppage. If the XFL and/or the AAF are willing to open their wallets a little, it could mean they peel off some of the bigger names, and maybe even a few fans, from the NFL.

It's just another reason one or both of the leagues could have staying power.

THE SPRING LEAGUE

The Spring League is the brainchild of Brian Woods, a football entrepreneur who has worked with several leagues and bowl games. It's a unique and innovative idea that is slowly gaining traction.

The basics: The league is made up of four teams of about 40 players each. Teams play a three-week schedule at one location to eliminate travel costs and keep lodging and food prices under control. In 2018, the league was held in Austin, Texas, an easier-to-reach location than somewhat remote White Sulphur Springs, W.Va., where it was held the first year. Unlike other leagues that pay the players, all participants must pay the league a fee ($700 in 2018) to play.

Wait . . . the players pay?: Yes. That's one of Woods' innovations. Believe it or not, that's a good thing. In most leagues, players seek agents to call around and try to find them opportunities because, frankly, it doesn't cost the player anything and it allows the player to put off the rest of his life. When you ask a player (or his agent) to pay his own way, you find out how badly he wants to pay professionally. It also takes a lot of the pressure off Woods as it's a really hard sell trying to find broadcast partners, sponsors and ticket buyers for alternative leagues.

The NFL pays attention: I'm not going to say The Spring League is a springboard (sorry) to the NFL, but I will say that teams have consistently sent pro scouts to watch the games during both of the league's first two seasons (the league also has a one-week "showcase" on the West Coast during the summer). There have been several players that have earned NFL tryouts based on their performances during Spring League play. That almost assuredly would not have happened if they had not been on league rosters. For those three weeks, all the league's players get a longer look than virtually any indoor league player gets over three months.

Growing credibility: One measure of any league's legitimacy is its talent level. In Year 1 of the Spring League, I think the main qualification for making a team was paying your money. However, Year 2 featured enigmatic and colorful QB **Johnny Manziel** as well as a handful of other players who had NFL experience. I think that as the league moves forward, it will attract more up-and-coming talent and fewer has-beens trying to hang on. I think the needle is definitely pointing up for the league.

THE AFL

The lights are growing dimmer on indoor football, but let's cover it anyway.

The upside of the AFL: First, let's talk about the pluses, and there's one very big one. If your son signs a CFL deal, he's obligated for two years unless he gets cut. Not so in the Arena League. In fact, if your son were to sign an AFL deal today, and tomorrow got offered a contract by an NFL team, he'd be free to go, no questions asked. Also, if your son is a quarterback, a position that requires longer gestation than most other positions, the league is a proven model for positive development. Remember, **Kurt Warner** once played in the league, and **Jay Gruden**, the Redskins head coach, came to the NFL directly from the AFL, though he never played in the league beyond spending time on practice squads.

The downside: The pay scale is the obvious negative to the league, especially since the AFL re-emerged from bankruptcy in 2010. As of 2015, veterans got paid $830 a week and rookies got paid $775 a week. In addition, the starting QB got a $250 start bonus each game. That may be OK for competitive softball, but it's pretty small potatoes for a game as violent as football in which players are risking their health on every snap.

So why play in the AFL?: If your son didn't get an NFL shot, he needs new film. The Arena League is one way to do that. The longer your son stays away from the game, the less relevant he becomes. Football is a unique game in that the only way to improve is to play.

Other indoor leagues: The Arena Football League is not the only indoor football in America, though it is probably the most stable league. It's also probably the best-paying, though other leagues are usually in the same ballpark. The big issue is that indoor football is a low-margin proposition, and that's especially true of leagues that lack sponsorship and a built-in fan base. Where there's no money, there's volatility. What's more, the AFL is probably the only indoor league NFL scouts bother with on an annual basis. Regional indoor leagues are mostly populated with people who just don't want to move on with their lives.

Afterword

I know there's a lot to know and plenty of obstacles as you help guide your son to a pro football career. I also know that there have many times in these pages that I've been pretty blunt about the odds facing him. I hope I haven't put too fine a point on it.

I chose the name www.succeedinfootball.com for my blog because that's also the credo for Inside the League.

I want your son to achieve his dreams. I want people to make it to the league, and if not to the league, at least to some form of football fulfillment. What's more, that fulfillment may not come from putting on the pads. There are so many jobs in football, and it's incredibly rewarding to make your living doing something you love, like I do. It's especially rewarding for us at ITL whenever we can make a positive impact on someone who's really going for it and trying to beat the odds by working in the game.

Before I go, I wanted to take this opportunity to wish your son luck in his football ventures. And if you're not a parent but someone that picked up this book in hopes of learning the ropes of the game, I wish you luck, as well. I also hope you'll reach out to us at Inside the League. We are dedicated to helping people like you get into the game in whatever way they seek.

Best of luck, and God bless you in whatever road you choose and whatever field you play on.

www.ingramcontent.com/pod-product-compliance
Lightning Source LLC
Chambersburg PA
CBHW061656040426
42446CB00010B/1767